Land of Our Father

Land of Our Father

◆

Land of Ours

A Story of Five Generations

Co-Authors
Erma Lois Cristeen (Britton) Moore
Rita Ann (Moore) King

iUniverse, Inc.
New York Lincoln Shanghai

Land of Our Father
Land of Ours

Copyright © 2005 by Rita King

iUniverse books may be ordered through booksellers or by contacting:

iUniverse
2021 Pine Lake Road, Suite 100
Lincoln, NE 68512
www.iuniverse.com
1-800-Authors (1-800-288-4677)

First Edition
Book cover by Janet Rose

ISBN: 0-595-34094-6

Printed in the United States of America

This book is dedicated to those who make up the glorious circle of twenty-four grandchildren of Hiram and Sarah Poe Britton. There were others, infants and little ones who did not live to grow up. Most of these twenty-four are now living with our Lord and their parents in heaven.

It is our hope that from reading this book, the children of these twenty-four will pause and write their story for their posterity.

Contents

INTRODUCTION

LAND OF OUR FATHER
LAND OF OURS

Erma Moore and Rita King—Summer 2001

Destination Alaska! Today we viewed the Denali National Park while enjoying a two-hour jet boat excursion on our 26 day adventure of Canada and Alaska in the summer of 2001. We celebrated Erma's 75th birthday as we arrived at our halfway point in the beautiful city of Anchorage, Alaska on July 19, 2001. The spectacular Alaska Range came out for us to see that day with Mt. McKinley peaking at over 20,000 feet. The mountain is the highest point in North America.

Summer 2004 we finally finished the book, "Land of Our Father; Land of Ours", we hope you enjoy this story of our family history. Watch in the coming years for our book titled "The Mountains have Come Out" which will tell of the love between a mother and daughter whose reach will be endless.

LAND OF OUR FATHER LAND OF OURS

The Life Story of George Arthur Britton and Bertha (Clark) Britton

INTRODUCTION

Erma Lois Cristeen (Britton) Moore
4th child of George A. and Bertha (Clark) Britton
Rita Ann (Moore) King
Granddaughter of George A. and Bertha (Clark) Britton
daughter of Erma and Herman Moore

In the summer of 2001, my mother Erma and I had the wonderful opportunity to plan and make a trip of a lifetime. We completed a round trip drive through the vast lands of western Canada and Alaska from Calgary, Alberta, Canada to Anchorage, Alaska. We covered over 4,800 miles in twenty-six days. We enjoyed fabulous scenery as we traveled over winding mountainous country roads and highways of upper North America. Most people may remember the main highway we traveled by its original name of the Alcan Highway. Today it is called the Alaskan Highway. This is a trip we would highly recommend. Even two young Indiana women such as we were can conquer the trip.

The time we spent together provided us with many hours for talking and reminiscing about our lives. I took a small handheld tape recorder and mom told me some of the wonderful stories of our early families and about her life growing up. As a result, we have taken the recordings along with notes from the past and put together this book for interesting family history reading. These personal memories and recollections have been compiled to remember our dear loved ones and is a special tribute to the life of George A. and Bertha (Clark) Britton. We have added some genealogical and historical research for more interesting reading.

We want to recognize and thank the many family members who have contributed their memories and stories to make this book "ours." We praise Jesus Christ for blessing us with a wonderful Christian heritage both from past ancestors and present living relatives.

The stories told in "Land of Our Father; Land of Ours" are from the memory of Erma (Britton) Moore and we've added others, too. Rita researched many old records and legal documents; however some records are lost forever. Together this project represents many hours of time and efforts.

1

The Early Family of George Arthur Britton

✦

Time period 1821–1915

This is my personal recollection of the life of my parents, **George Arthur Britton** and **Bertha (Clark) Britton**. My name is Erma Lois Cristeen (Britton) Moore.

I want to give a special thanks to my daughter, Rita Ann (Moore) King whose efforts have brought this story to paper and memories set in time. Genealogy is a continuing study of family history and we have focused on writing more about people instead of dates and times. This book will help document the stories behind our early pioneer families and our generation which is known as the Greatest Generation.

It gives me great pleasure to live my life in the fullest now in my seventies and enjoying good health. The Britton and Poe stories are memories I have always wanted to put in a personal book. Some memories of stories take us back as early as the 1800's.

For the most part this Britton story will be told in a chronological order from the life of George Arthur Britton.

George Arthur Britton was born the 3rd son of Hiram Pierce Britton and Sarah Elizabeth (Poe) Britton on July 20, 1884 in Pendleton County, Kentucky. The story begins with the families of the Britton's and the Poe's who were living in Ohio and Kentucky in the middle 1800's.

Hiram Pierce Britton father of George A. Britton was born in Aberdeen, Ohio in Brown County on December 28, 1859. Hiram P Britton was from a family of 12 children born to Martin Watson Britton and Lucretia A. (Frame) Britton who made their home in Brown County, Ohio. Martin W. Britton and Lucretia A. Frame were married in Brown County, Ohio February 14, 1844.

Martin Watson Britton father of Hiram P. Britton was born April 18, 1821 in Ohio. Lucretia A. (Frame) Britton, mother of Hiram was born November 11, 1827 in Ohio. Martin and Lucretia Britton are buried the I.O.O.F. cemetery located in Lenoxburg, Kentucky. We just recently found their grave sites. The grave headstone reveals Lucretia died in the year 1890. She died October 13, 1890. It appears Martin's death date is not on the headstone but we have no reason to believe he is not also buried there beside Lucretia.

Martin Watson Britton was a logger and cleared timber off of the land. I don't remember much about Martin and Lucretia as Grandpa Hiram didn't speak to often of his parents. The twelve children of Martin and Lucretia were vaguely recalled by Hiram and only "Aunt Annie" as I remember him stating was a woman of small stature. She was the next child born after Hiram. She lived to be over ninety years of age. This picture was taken in 1937 at Sharon Woods Park; Cincinnati, Ohio at a Britton family reunion.

Left to right: Victor Eugene Britton b. 9-25-1864 "Uncle Vic", Martina Ann (Anna) (Britton) Yates b. 6-14-1862 "Aunt Annie", Grandpa Hiram Pierce Britton, and Emmett Martin Britton b. 4-24-1857 "Uncle Mett".

Victor Britton, Anna (Britton) Yates, Hiram Britton, Emmett Britton

We are still researching the family Britton line before Martin Watson Britton and some feel certain that Martin's fathers name was Joseph Britton and his mother's name was Nancy (Watson) Britton. Someday those who study genealogy will make the connection that at some point in time we all came from across the oceans from other lands.

Sarah Elizabeth (Poe) Britton mother of George A. Britton was born February 11, 1860 in Pendleton County, Kentucky. Sarah's family was from Caddo, Kentucky. She was one of twelve children, a daughter of Elizabeth (Cummings) Poe and William Brittain Poe. Sarah's father was born in Bracken County, Kentucky and her mother was born in Pendleton County, Kentucky.

Families in the late 1800's all usually lived close by each other and many times worked in the same occupations. The Poe's and the Britton's were families who logged timber and floated the logs down the Ohio River. In Aberdeen, Ohio and Maysville, Kentucky the land was still in the virgin timber and the hills were covered with many trees. The timber industry was big in those days and demand for wood was high. Many businesses and employment opportunities were born out of the prosperity of harvesting the timber for wood.

The Ohio River was used for transporting the huge cuts of timber. Often times the large timbers were rolled down from the surrounding hillsides of Ohio and Kentucky and into the Ohio River which flowed past the towns of Aberdeen and Maysville. Cincinnati is about 60 miles northwest from Aberdeen and was the major receiving point for timber. The story is told that the loggers would wait until the level of the river would rise then just as the water level begin to recede the loggers would drop the loads of timber along with their flatboats into the river and head off towards Cincinnati for processing.

We would just image the river was at times a fast moving hazard for people and boats traveling. The Poe family had a tradition of taking a bell with them when they would cross the Ohio River. When they would reach the opposite side of the river they would ring the bells so their loved ones across the river would know they made it safely to shore.

The loggers were a rowdy bunch of men who were known for being strong people with tall statures, especially the Britton's. The logging work required tough and brute strength. The Britton's had big hands and the story is told by family members that once a Britton man killed a man with his bare hands after finding out that his wife had been unfaithful. I tell you this story because I want you to know the Britton's were very strong people. They say this Britton man moved west and never was prosecuted.

The timber industry was good and boomed during World War I, but when the economy faded, log prices began to drop and many logging companies went out of business. Nationally the period of downsizing came about 1919–1921.

Working in the timber business Hiram Britton worked and lived in about the same vicinity as Sarah Poe in Caddo, Kentucky. When Hiram and Sarah began their courtship he was 17 years old and she was 16 years old. They would walk on the road and sing songs together. They would sing at the Methodist Church and give their testimonies of their love for The Lord. Hiram was a big strong, determined, severe, methodical man and he ruled very keenly. Sarah was a beautiful, quiet, angelical type person. She was a jewel of a rare kind. Hiram and Sarah were married September 8, 1878 at the Pine Grove Church in Pendleton County, Kentucky.

Sarah Elizabeth (Poe) Britton & Hiram Pierce Britton Wedding Day 1878

Hiram and Sarah continued to live in Pendleton County, Kentucky after they were married. Hiram loved the Lord and served as a music director and taught Sunday school classes in churches throughout his life. Sarah was a fine Christian woman and enjoyed taking her children to church and raising them in the nurture of a Christian home.

Some of the early settlements of Pendleton County, Kentucky were being chartered as early as 1792 such as Falmouth. Other settlements were known as Boston Station (1790), Grassy Creek, Fort Lick, Snake Creek, Flour Creek, Caldwell Station, Catawba, Gardnersville, and Wampum to name a few.

Businesses varied from settlement to settlement in the early Kentucky towns. There were general stores, buggy shops, blacksmiths, millinery shops, sewing machine dealers, barbers, saloons, tobacco warehouses, saw mills, lumber and mining, milk hauling, doctors, and community halls. There were churches, schools, and post offices.[1]

Hiram and Sarah's first child was named James Elmer Britton who was born August 12, 1879. William Howard Britton was born October 8, 1881; George

Arthur Britton was born July 20, 1884, Rosa Nell born May 7, 1886, and Elsie May Britton born August 11, 1888. All five of these children were born in the area of Pendleton County, Kentucky. I remember some of their nick names; James was (Elmer), William was (Howard) and Rosa was (Nellie). Over the nine years that Hiram and Sarah's first 5 children were born the source of the families income came from the logging industry.

◆   ◆   ◆

In 1889 three million acres of Indian Territory in Oklahoma was opened up for people of the United State to claim homestead land. Hiram Britton and some of the Poe family men decided to set out for Oklahoma in hopes of staking homesteads land sites for their families. Travel was hard for those who went mostly by horses and covered wagons. Railroads provided access for some. When Hiram and the Poe's made their way west they discovered that many, many people were already ahead of them on the line to cross over and claim land. They decided to turn back and went back to Kentucky. The trip was the farthest west Hiram Britton would ever venture. History records the "run" for farms and town lots brought over ten thousand people in the first day to the Oklahoma lands. Several months before the official April 22, 1889 opening of the land, people worked as federal marshals, railroad personnel and other legal representatives. These representatives were prohibited from claiming land, but it was learned that some of these people made claim to land sites illegally. They were called "legal sooners". Many problems arose for individuals who made attempts to claim out one of the 160-acres homesteads. The land rush lasted several years, but Hiram and the Poe's returned back home to Kentucky within weeks after their departure.[2]

Just as families stayed together in areas they also moved together as families. The Poe's stayed together and the Britton's moved 80 miles south to Fleming County, Kentucky. Sarah was 7 1/2 months pregnant when they made their trip to Fleming County in a spring wagon. Just months later, on October 31, 1890, their sixth child Dempsey Carroll Britton was born. Hiram continued to work in the logging industry.

My father George Britton was a young boy when the family made this move. It was in Fleming County that George learned basic math, geography, states and capitals, water ways in America and acquired a broad knowledge of the world. He wrote with a slate pencil using a slate board and was a very good reader.

Hiram and Sarah several years later moved westward about 80 miles to Scott County and farmed in a nice bluegrass section of Georgetown, Kentucky.

This is when Hiram starting in the farming occupation. Grace Ellen Britton was born there on October 18, 1895. Grace Britton was the fair haired sister of my father who everyone dearly loved.

Again Hiram's family was on the move from Scott County, Kentucky to Owen County, Kentucky where the family continued farming. It was in Owen County that Walter Ford Britton was born on November 14, 1897. Hiram and Sarah purchased a farm the next year in the spring of 1898. The land was poor with many rocky hills which made farming more difficult. The house was located on a hillside with a creek running at the bottom of the hill. We don't know exactly why the family choose Owenton, Kentucky but as time past Owen County would be remembered as a very sad place not just for farming but events that would pierce the very heart of a family.

The boys were growing up and almost everything was done by hand with a lot of physical work. Wood needed to be cut for firewood. George cut wood and helped to take care of the family. George was the frailest of the boys. Hiram Britton was so busy working the farm and raising his family he failed many times to attend church regularly.

Many say that when you begin to live life as though you don't need God or don't have time for Him this can lead to hard times without protection to yourself and your family. It was during this period that awful tragedies begin to happen to the children of Hiram and Sarah.

Life on a farm in the county often lured the passion of young boys to get out on their own and hunt the land. The Britton boys were no exception to the sport. They enjoyed the freedom and bounty of a good hunting day. The story goes that Howard had received a new gun of which he was proud. Howard carrying his new gun headed off with his brother Elmer for a Sunday morning of hunting. While walking along the creek two black boys approached the brothers seeking to admire the new gun of Howard's. One of the boys reached out to take the gun out of Howard's hand and the boys scuffled. Howard was defensive to his new gun.

As the fight began the gun accidentally shot straight in the direction of Howard's brother Elmer. Elmer was shot in the head. He lived unconscious in their home for one night and died the next day at the age of nineteen years old. Grandma Sarah had lost her firstborn son.

Hiram was very angry at Howard and turned his mourning against him. It wasn't long after Elmer's death that Howard couldn't stand to be in Owenton and he traveled about 30 miles south where some of Sarah's people were living. It was in this move that Howard learned the skills of a carpenter.

Time would pass and on May 5, 1902 the last child of Hiram and Sarah would be born in Owen County. Her name was Lora Dell Britton, a precious little girl who would warm the hearts of all the family. Little did the family know that heartache would hit them again this time with the life of Hiram and Sarah's last child, Lora Dell.

A sickness known as the Flux was hitting the young children very hard in the area. Most children survived the intestinal infection. Sadly Lora Dell contracted the Flux and within a few days died on July 31, 1903. She was barely over fourteen months old. Death was too much in Owenton for the Hiram Britton family.

We found records at the I.O.O. F. Cemetery in Owenton, Kentucky of Hiram's purchase of a cemetery lot in 1898. We don't have any official month of Elmer's death but we believe the year was 1898. We found the funeral record for Lora Dell which helped us find the cemetery where Elmer was buried. There were no headstones for either grave and in July 2003 on the 100th year of Lora Dell's death we placed a beautiful pink stone with their names carved in memory James Elmer Britton and Lora Dell Britton the 1st born and last born children of Hiram and Sarah Britton.

The picture shown below was taken at the end of the summer of 1903 in Owenton, Kentucky and is the family of H.P. Britton on their farm. Photographs were rarely taken because it was considered a luxury most families could not afford. The photographer would come to the home and take family pictures. Left to right on the back row is Nellie, George and Elsie. Nellie and Elsie were tall and they were wearing white floor length embroidered dresses with high collars sometimes referred to as a bertha. George was nineteen years old in this picture wearing his hat. Left to right on the first row is Hiram, Grace, Dempsey, Walter, and Sarah. Hiram dressed in his work clothes sitting on a chair, as the small children are posing straight faces, with Sarah and her heavy laden sad face.

The family had suffered two tragic family deaths and the toll taken was written on the face of Sarah who appeared much older than her 43 years of age. It was time for the family to move on. I suspect Sarah never returned to her children's grave sites, mostly because families didn't travel much in those days and the hurt could be too much to bear.

The Britton House in Owen County Kentucky
Front row Hiram Pierce, Grace, Dempsey, Walter, & Sarah Elizabeth
Back row Nellie, George & Elsie

Life in America in the early 20th Century was busy as our nation was learning about new modern society and consumers needs and wants. I want to tell you about some of the events, trends, and lifestyles during the early 1900's that filled people leisure time and satisfied their changing styles. There were melodrama and cheap seats in theaters and concert halls, saloons, dance halls, pool rooms, roller-skating rinks, circuses, amusement parks, burlesque shows, and professional sports. Fashionable clothing and sheet music of popular songs were mass produced. Billboard advertising was popular and they urged people to buy. There were old fashion department stores and mail order selling. In 1900 the Brownie camera was introduced to America and also the button-down shirt. In 1903 the Wright Brothers took their 1st flight in their invented plane and The Ford Motor Co. was founded. The first radio broadcast came in 1904. In 1913 the use of an electric refrigerator came to America. I find it interesting to read the history of our country's progress throughout decades especially when these are the things happening in the time period of our story being told.[3]

In reality for the Brittons and the Poes being rural farmers and laborers the families didn't travel very often. When they did travel it was by way of their horses, wagons, and buggies. Entertainment and lifestyles were enjoyed by the family through simple activities such as family picnics and swimming in the river. The farming occupation required farmers to work from daylight to dark to accomplish all the chores that needed to be done on the farm. Occasionally the rural towns sponsored street fairs and county fairs in which the rural people would participate. Even though industry and trends were rapidly changing within larger towns the rural communities progressed at a slower pace.

The Owenton farm was sold in 1904 and the Britton family moved to Hamilton, Ohio located about 60 miles northeast of Owenton, Kentucky. My father had gone earlier to this growing area of Ohio. Some of the Poe families lived there and industry provided employment. Hamilton was a fun place to live with industry, business and work for those who wanted to work. Dad worked as a machinist in a paper mill. He admitted there were times when it was hard for him to get up early for work in the town. Living on the farm in Owen County he could sleep into the morning hours and start his work later on in the day. Most of the other Britton family men ended up working in Hamilton; Dempsey a machinist, Howard and Hiram worked as laborers.

Hamilton at the time still had a lot of virgin land with excellent rabbit hunting as I recall dad telling stories about the area. Even today in the Hamilton/Fairview area of Ohio lives the first born granddaughter of George Britton; Sharon (Britton) Depoi.

Dad was happy to see his beautiful younger sisters in an area where they could get a good education. It was in Hamilton that Nellie and Elsie met their husbands to be and they married there, too. Nellie married Robert E. Grimes on May 9, 1907. Elsie married Frank Lamb on February 5, 1910.

Howard married Ollie May (Newkirk) on February 16, 1910. Since the story doesn't go into much more details of Howard and Ollie we report that they enjoyed 58 years of marriage before Howard died on April 15, 1968 and Ollie died a few years later in 1977.

George attended a Methodist Church in Hamilton. It was here that he put his faith in Jesus Christ as his personal Savior and began his walk of service and dedication to The Lord Jesus Christ. We found the church recently which is now named Cornerstone.

Cornerstone Apostolic Church—Hamilton, Ohio 2003

My father prayed for all his future family to be followers and believers in Christ Jesus and believed that Christianity is the truth. Jesus said in the Bible, "I am the way and the truth and the life" in John 14: 6 and we must enter heaven through believing in Jesus. Romans 3: 23 says for all of us have sinned and have fallen short of the glory of God. Not one of us is perfect. The Bible also tells us that the wages (price we pay) of sin is death; Romans 6: 23, but if we believe in Jesus our gift is eternal life.

Salvation is a simple act of accepting Jesus and believing the penalty for our sins are paid through the blood Jesus Christ shed when He died on the cross for all of us. Galatians 2:20 When we accept and believe this we become Children of God and Heaven is our eternal home if we are faithful to the end of our lives. George loved to tell the story of Jesus and His love for everyone. He was a young man now and visited the local jail with his preacher and told prisoners about Jesus, God and the Bible. It was these years that George knew that God had surely called him into the ministry.

The family continued to live in Hamilton several more years. This picture of Sarah and Hiram was taken in Hamilton, Ohio around 1908.

Grandpa Hiram and Grandma Sarah had dreams of owning their own farm land again. Hiram wanted to grow tobacco which was a very profitable crop. Some of the Poe's and Britton's had moved to Connersville, Indiana. Sarah's brother George Andrew Poe and his wife Eva (Hurd) Poe "Uncle George and Aunt Evie" lived in a little house up on Georgia Avenue in Connersville. They attended church at the Nazarene Church. They always lived in town. They were not farmers.

December 20, 1910 Grandpa Hiram bought an 88.59 acre farm on top of Egypt Hill, right at the corner of Fayette, Union, and Franklin counties in Indiana. The farm had a log house but Hiram built a better house on the land. There were other Brittons who lived around the same area and some Poe families lived on Duck Creek.

The Egypt Hill farm later became known as the Egypt Hollow farm. Grandpa Hiram believed he could get rich on tobacco. He joined what was called The Grange which was a forerunner of the Farm Bureau. The farmers met at Everton, Indiana to talk about getting the prices up for farm products. The market had fallen on tobacco and there was no value in the tobacco crop that Grandpa Hiram had just put out. That's when he gave up raising tobacco and switched over to raising corn and wheat. These products were sold around the Connersville, Brookville and Rushville, Indiana areas. Tobacco wasn't raised in Indiana like it was in Kentucky.

I just have to add this about the Egypt Hollow Farm as I remember it as a child. I only remember the last years Grandpa Hiram and Grandma Sarah lived there as I was one of the younger grandchildren. It was always a wonderful time for me when we went to visit there. Aunt Grace was always there with them and I believe that she was a big determiner of how things would go around there. To me, she could have been an international diplomat, but she used her skills and talents on the farm life. The house had cement sidewalks all around it and they were bordered by a small wine colored plant, and things were always in place. Aunt Grace loved flowers, sewing and making rugs and lovely things. She was only fifteen years old when she came to Indiana and lived on the Egypt Hollow Farm until she was in her early 40's. The house was always spotless, and every inch was swept clean, inside and out. Even the wide cellar steps leading down into the basement were clean.

Driving down the lane which made a left turn towards the house was planted an apple orchard with trees standing parallel in two straight rows for about 500 feet. Behind the woodshed was a second fruit orchard, planted with lovely pear, peach, and plum trees of different varieties. The front orchard was of fall and winter apples which would last all winter. I can imagine Aunt Grace pouring over the catalogs deciding which trees and other things to order for planting. The garden was planted with a wide variety of vegetables, boysenberries, strawberries and cherry trees. All of this was preserved in the spotless cellar for winter use. There was a smoke house where Grandpa cured the meat of the animals butchered in the fall. It too was spotless and smelled oh, so good!

Next to the smokehouse was the woodshed filled with chips from the many cuttings. It was here the dogs stayed in the winter. Of course there were chicken houses and eggs and a big barn where we climbed in the rafters. The only place we couldn't play was the granary, a big room lined with wonderful wood where Grandpa stored the wheat, it awaiting a higher market price to be sold. This farm really showed that these people cared about it.

Everything seemed ample and providential to me. We loved to go and eat at Grandma's table. Sarah's family came to join at many of the Sunday dinners. The children would play games and hike through the woods. It was always fun at Grandma's. The only thing about memories as a child is that time goes too fast and we are soon thrust into making a life of our own.

Aunt Grace had several suitors, but she decided not to marry. She said she spent much of her time caring for her nieces and nephews. She drove for the family and worked as the bookkeeper for the farms. She had a ski suit from the catalog to stay warm in winter long before women started wearing slacks. She had beautiful clothes. I can remember her black velvet coat with an ermine fur (white) cape collar, her blue lace gown and once she ordered a peach colored knit dress, a new thing made out of corn stocks. I guess that never caught on, it was the only one I ever saw. She was very beautiful and especially loved by everyone.

George eventually left the Hamilton, Ohio area to follow the rest of the family who by 1910 had moved into the Fairfield and Everton areas of Franklin, Union and Fayette Counties of Indiana. The children of Hiram and Sarah were young adults now starting their own families and grandchildren were being born. George didn't choose to marry young and it wouldn't be long now until he would find himself on a journey to Canada.

2

Young Pioneer Man in the Canadian Wilderness

❖

1915–1917

In the warm season of 1915, my father set out for the Canadian Wilderness in Kelvington, Saskatchewan, Canada. The reason he did this was Frank Lamb, George's brother-in-law wanted to investigate an opportunity to receive free land. Canada was offering free homesteads for people who would set up households, clear and develop virgin wilderness land plots. Frank Lamb had British background and Canada is very British. He was an entrepreneur afraid of nothing and wanted to claim a homestead in Canada.

In 1872 Canada established a law that encouraged the settlement of Canada's Prairie Provinces. It was called The Dominion Land Acts. Dad's homestead was in the Province of Saskatchewan in Township 38, of the 2nd Meridian, section 20 and was 159 acres. A homesteader paid a $10 fee and agreed to cultivate at least 30 acres and build a house (often just a sod house) within three years; then the homesteader gained a title to the land.[4]

Grandmother Sarah wanted George to go with Frank and Elsie and help oversee the adventure. My father was in his early thirties and single when they all packed up to leave. Frank and Elsie had a young daughter named Ethel Grace who was about four years of age. They went by train we believe from Chicago to Winnipeg, Canada. They then changed to another train that took them on a 400 mile northwestern route to their final destination, Wadena Saskatchewan, Canada. Dad told me that the only thing he took with him was a manufactured fold-up stove. He believed he could make his own furniture but didn't think he could make a stove.

When they arrived in Wadena, they went to the land office to apply for their homestead. Daddy and Frank each received a 160 acre tract of land. Daddy's land bordered on a lake and there was quit a large area of marshland in his section. There was a lean-to on it built by a previous owner who had turned the land back into the land office. Most would say Daddy's land wasn't a real true homestead property since it had been previously occupied. George cleared more of the land and kept it nice. The yard around the house was cleared; a rail fence surrounded the yard and close by was a barn.

Dad had a cow for milk and horses.

The land was about 10 miles from the town of Kelvington. To get there, he took the road out of town heading north for approximately 5 miles to a T-road. At the T, he turned right (east) and traveled another 4 miles to his property.

My brother Gordon and I took a trip to Kelvington in 1990 to visit the area where our father had lived. The little lean-to had been replaced by a little square house with a bonnet roof (a round roof that was pointed in the middle). That probably would have been where the smoke would go out of the house. There was a well located inside the house. This was good because it kept the well from freezing even in the coldest of the wintertime so daddy would always have water.

While in Saskatchewan we met a fine lady Mrs. Ida Moss who owned the homestead property that had been owned by our father, George when he lived in Canada. She showed us records from the early beginnings of the 640 acre homestead plot.

In the 1950's, Ida and her husband had built a country store and a post office was established there in the area. Ida was given charge of the records that were part of the history of the little school that my mother, Bertha and father, George had been instrumental in establishing. The schoolhouse provided room for approximately 25–30 school aged children. In fact Ida showed us school board meetings documents where George had served as secretary and President of the school board. Later in time my mother, Bertha served as secretary. I'll give more details of that period in time later in the story.

The winters in Canada got extremely cold with the temperatures going down to 35 degrees below zero and 70 degrees below was not uncommon. Depending on the time of the year, the trip into town would vary. The lakes and ponds would freeze over allowing you to cross either by using snow shoes and walking or riding a horse. One particular time, George went into town walking across the frozen lake that bordered his land. While he was in town for a couple of days, the weather moderated and the lake became unsafe to cross so he would have to walk around the lake which took many more hours to complete the journey.

It was getting dark and he realized that it would be necessary for him to find shelter for the night as it was still a very cold winter night. Fortunately, he noticed a cottage and went up to ask for shelter. It is a rule of the wilderness country to open your house to anyone who needs shelter from the cold. A woman and her two children were home and opened the door for my father, a man they didn't even know and allowed him to stay overnight. These were the customs.

Visible in the cold winter nights at times if you looked towards the northern Canadian sky you could see the Aurora borealis (Northern Lights). My father told me of how beautiful the luminous atmospheric phenomenon can be when you go outside and look up and see the many colors that make up this display. Many times daddy would witness the wonders of these rapidly shifting patches of dancing hues of light.

One winter Dad decided to do some logging to help break up the monotony of the lonely prairie. The head of the logging company said to him, "well, you are quite small to do this heavy work, but we do need a cook." "Can you cook?" Daddy said "yes." For one season, he cooked for the logging crew. It was tiring job but at least he wasn't alone.

My father had several books he read and studied during the years he lived by himself while in Canada. His favorites included a collection of Shakespeare and the Holy Bible. He believed the Bible is God's divine truth for us and he loved to learn more about the Bible. He studied it extensively and memorized many of the scriptures, an effort that would prove to serve him well in latter life.

My father was a spiritual man and held a deep love for the Lord Jesus Christ he was always eager to know more about Jesus who he loved with all his heart. Everywhere he would go he wanted to learn more about the Bible and share it with others. It wasn't long after he arrived in Canada that he noticed a schoolhouse located just a few miles down the road from his land. The white building would be perfect for a Sunday church service. He opened the building and shortly had a congregation of 30–40 people gathering for church services. Here is a picture of him kneeling in the front-left side with his congregation.

1917 George's Canadian Church family

The Lamb's land was located about 3 miles west from the T road or about 6 miles from my father. There were a few more settlements in their area than in Daddy's. Frank did not farm his land but traveled the area and sold supplies to the settlers. Later they moved to a new property at the corner of the T road where he started raising cattle. Frank and Elsie had three children. A daughter Ethel came with them from Indiana. The two boys were born in Canada. John Russell was born on April 1, 1916 and Frank Gilbert was born in 1919.

Log home of Frank and Elsie Lamb 1919 in Canada

Frank and Elsie's family 1921

The Lambs lived in Canada several more years before returning to United States. We would love to tell you more about their adventures in Canada but we haven't had an opportunity to gather very many of their stories.

After Elsie and Frank's first son John Russell was born in the spring of 1916, Elsie began to miss her home and family back in Indiana. She wrote her sister Nellie encouraging her to come north to Canada and set up their own homestead. Nellie and her husband Robert Edward Grimes decided to make the adventure into the wilds of Canada and claim a homestead for themselves. They left from Franklin County, Indiana with three small daughters who were all under school age. The young girls' names were Mary Evelyn, Elsie Roberta and Florence Edna.

Roberta (Grimes) Rush tells these stories. "My parents traveled in a jolt wagon during the springtime with the children wrapped up in blankets to keep them warm. We arrived at the train station; I was about two years old. A black man who worked for the railroad helping people load their bag, reached down to pick me up. I broke loose and ran. My dad almost didn't catch up with me as I was a fast runner".

The Grimes were issued out their own homestead land. The property was very near to the land occupied by Frank and Elsie Lamb. They lived in a log sodden roof cabin. Roberta remembers her father telling of the time when a piece of sod fell off of the roof and hit her in the head. She recalls, "Dad thought it had killed me but of course it didn't." Even thought Roberta was only three years old she distinctively remembers seeing an Indian Pow-Wow (a social gathering of the Indians) where a deer ran across the front yard.

Florence was just over one year old when the family made their move to the North County. Roberta said she helped to teach her younger sister Florence to walk by encouraging her to walk across the floor in the family's log cabin.

Robert and Nellie only stayed one year with their family in Canada. "Nellie said she couldn't raise her little girls in the wilderness of Canada without a doctor or medical help," recalled Roberta. "It was a hard way to live in the thickness of mosquitoes and the uncertainty of the winter weather. In the winter you would have to tie a rope to your barn from the house otherwise if a winter storm blew in you wouldn't be able to find the barn for the white out caused by a blizzard. In the warm season living in Canada with all the mosquitoes many times your family would build a fire just outside the cabin. When the family would return home from their travels they would go through the smoke before they would enter the cabin. This way the mosquitoes wouldn't come along with them inside the cabin."

The Grimes family returned home to Indiana where they would raise their children. A fourth child whose name was Harold Grimes was born at the Egypt Hollow farm. Robert's occupation was farming but he also worked as a guard in a local factory for a time. They enjoyed fifty-three years of marriage until Robert died in September 1960. Nellie died August 1976 in Fayette County, Indiana. They are both buried in the Britten plot at the Dale Cemetery in Connersville, Indiana.

The story of the Indian Chief and his daughter was a story we remember daddy telling us. On the northern side of the lake that bordered my father's land there was an Indian Reservation. The Indian men came by the lake riding their horses to the nearby town of Kelvington. Many times when daddy would go to Kelvington he noticed the Indians along the streets and buildings just sitting there. The Indians never talked to anyone. They were known to stay for several days. When the Indian men were ready to return home with their supplies they would leave in a pack of about 4 or 5 on their horses.

George was known to work very diligently in his fields. And the Indians as they passed by traveling on their way would observe George. My father told me that one day the Indian Chief rode his horse down by where he was working and right behind him on a pony was the Indian Chief's beautiful daughter. She was dressed and adorned with all the regalia of the Indian tribe. The Indian Chief wore his beautiful head feathers. Their dress was of the beautiful colors that the Indians were known for wearing when they enjoyed ceremonial celebrations. As they slowly approached, George realized that it was in the mind of the Indian Chief to give his daughter to him. It was at this time daddy realized it was time to return home to search for a wife of his choosing.

World War I had begun in about 1914. Austria had declared war on Serbia. Many European powers were at war during these years of WWI. George knew that returning to the United States might mean that he would be sent over to Europe to fight in the war. About 1917 was when my father decided at age 33 it was time for him to go back to Connersville in hopes of finding a wife.

3

A Courtship and Wedding

❖

1918–Spring 1920

Hiram and Sarah were still farming down on Egypt Hollow when George returned home from Canada. Their farm was about a 12 mile drive from The First Church of the Nazarene which at that time was on 4th Street in Connersville. The Pentecostal Church of the Nazarene as it was first called was established around 1910. Hiram and Sarah attended as regularly as possible.

Church life was not only enrichment for the souls but very much a part of the social life in the community. Grandma Sarah's brother Rev. George Poe and his wife Eva were charter members of the Nazarene Church. Both families contributed to the early growth within the church. When George returned to Connersville he noticed many new faces attending at The Nazarene Church. Among some of the new families included were the Clark girls whose names were Ruby, Bessie, Bertha, and Rosa. Bertha was about 22 years of age at this time and her sisters were already married.

In those days congregations liked to do things together such as gather for Sunday afternoon church meeting. The Bentley Church (Bentley Rd. 2 miles east of Everton) was often the place for gatherings for it was a beautiful area in the summertime for being outdoors.

Before George left for Canada, he had been attending a Methodist church in Blooming Grove. The church was located south of Connersville on State Road 1 and was closer to the Egypt Hollow farm. Dad had helped in the farming before his journey to Canada.

Several of the local churches were planning an all day summertime service at The Bentley Church. Everyone drove and met there. Grandpa Hiram and Grandma Sarah's farm was only 2 more miles east of the Bentley Road and George decided to attend this special day. Among the people attending on the beautiful sunny summer day were Bertha Clark and Lloyd Lynn. Mr. Lynn was a nice young single man. Bertha and Lloyd were good friends. They were never romantically involved.

Bertha was a small boned woman with long brownish black hair. Her skin was olive in color and she was very beautiful. When George met her he immediately took a liking to her. He took her away from Lloyd Lynn that day and Lloyd Lynn didn't have a girl the rest of the day. Dad had met Bertha Clark and they would go on to be married in a few years.

In 1918 the Britton family enjoyed attending church and owned a car.

World War I had ended and Grandpa Hiram had driven the car to town. In all of the excitement of the victory in Europe the town's people were celebrating. Someone hit Grandpa's car from behind and when he returned home he told everyone that was the last time he would ever drive a car. He was serious and his daughter Grace took over driving for the family. Grace already had experience driving and had taken the children to school at Egypt Hollow in the spring wagon Later Grace acquired a nice touring car with large front seats, 2 seats in back and additional 2 seats behind that. She drove the children to school in Everton, Indiana. She was no doubt one of the first lady school bus drivers in the USA. Grace was good at many things and kept the bookkeeping for the Britton farms.

The Clarks moved to Connersville from Cincinnati, Ohio about 1887 and would become part of our family tree line. Albert Clark and Emma Mae (Fick) were married on August 6, 1887. We still haven't been able to find their marriage record, but most of the family believes they were married in Cincinnati, Ohio. Albert and Emma are the parents of Bertha (Clark) Britton. We did find and confirm that Alexander Clark (Albert's father) died in Connersville, Indiana on March 27, 1887. During the civil war, we found that Alexander served in the 153rd Ohio Infantry. He died of disease of the throat and lungs.

He is buried in the Connersville City Cemetery in an unmarked grave.[5]

When Albert and Emma moved to Connersville, Albert built a little house on 934 W.16th Street. The girls began to attend the Nazarene as young women and would walk to the church which was just a little over a mile from their house. Albert and Emma also had three sons who were named, Howard, Elmer, and Arbie. The oldest of their children was Annie Elizabeth Clark who was only 2 years of age when she died in Connersville on February 10, 1890. Her real name was Margaret A. Clark.

Bertha was seventeen years old when she was employed by professional and industrial families in Connersville around 1913. Her occupation was a maid. She worked for the McKennan family taking care of their little seven year old girl who had long brown curly hair. Mr. McKennan managed the Maxine Company (dental supplies) which was located at 102 Heinemann Bldg. Bertha learned to cook wonderful meals. She learned how to make bread, fancy sauces and how to serve meals with all the correct etiquette. Bertha could never eat with the family but stayed in the kitchen and served the family their meals.

Howard worked at the Roots Blower Company which was only about one block down the street from where they lived on 16th Street. Howard was only 13 years old when he started employment at Roots, before there were child labor laws as we know of today. He learned the trade of tool and die and became a skilled precision instrument man.

Bertha was single in her early 20's when she applied for employment at the Spicely Drug Store which was located at 1502 Grand Avenue. She worked three years there making wonderful things like milkshakes and ice-cream deserts at the drug stores soda fountain.

Business was going good, Connersville in the early 1900's was known as "Little Detroit". The Automobile Manufacturers Association lists ten cars that called Connersville home: Central, 1905; McFarlan, 1900–1926; Lexington, 1910–1926; Empire, 1912–1919; Howard, 1914; Kelsey Cycle Car, 1913–1914; Van Auken Electric, 1914; Anstead, 1926; Auburn, 1929–1937; and Cord, 1936–1937. This information is from Connersville a Pictorial History that was written by Harry M. Smith a greatly admired local historian.[6]

Bertha's father Albert was diagnosed in having Huntington Chorea a degenerative nerve disease that results in uncontrollable body movements followed by mental deterioration. As years continued in his life he became an angry person who was very hard to live with. Emma couldn't live with Albert any longer and she divorced sometime later and moved to the Rush County, Indiana area. It was August 1, 1918 that Albert ended his own life in a horrible way by setting himself on fire and died almost immediately. Unfortunately Bertha and her brother Howard would witness the incident as it happened in the backyard at the little 16th Street house. Albert is buried in an unmarked grave at the Connersville City Cemetery on the north side middle area close to the fence next to the alley. He was 61 years old.

It had been earlier the same summer when George met Bertha in the Sunday afternoon gathering. My Grandmother, Emma Mae who now was married to her second husband Marshall Kirk and living down in Columbia Township said to Bertha, "Haven't you married him yet? Why don't you marry this nice man?" George Britton was 12 years older than Bertha. Just for the records Emma (Fick) and Riley Marshall Kirk were married in Rushville, Indiana on April 6, 1912. Many years later, Howard Clark showed us the little home they lived in near Columbia in Fayette County. He and his brothers were just children then.

It was in the fall 1918 Bertha went to Cincinnati, Ohio. She would attend God's Bible School, work, and socialize with Christian people at the school. Bertha needed a place to heal and recover from the loss of her father, Albert. The women wore long dresses with big hats. It was the Victorian age and women often dressed very classy with long gloves. The people at God's Bible School dressed very well with nice clothes.

There was a worldwide Influenza (flu) epidemic high point in 1918. More people were hospitalized in W.W.I from influenza than from wounds in the U.S. Army. The death rate was 80% at many of the medical WW1 facilities.

George Britton was fearful that Bertha living in Cincinnati and attending God's Bible School being a delicate fragile woman might die if she contacted the flu. He then realized he needed to go and get her. He went to Cincinnati by train to bring her home. This was probably in the fall of 1919.

It was in the spring of 1920 that Bertha decided to marry this preacher man, George. He was a God inspired Christian man who was very knowledgeable in the Holy Scriptures. Bertha enjoyed his company and loved when he would talk about the Bible with its many teachings and lessons.

Bertha became saved when she was seventeen. It was on that day she began to live her life in God's will and continued to serve Him all the days of her life. George and Bertha had a common faith and love for Jesus Christ. They were married on March 25, 1920 in the parsonage of the Nazarene church which was situated at that time on the corner of 5th & Western in Connersville. As we look at the house today it would be catty corner from the Salvation Army Church. The Rev. Johnnie Wilson conducted the ceremony. A formal photo was taken of only mother and dad the day they were married.

Bertha (Clark) Britton and George A. Britton on their Wedding Day 1920

Hiram and Sarah had purchased a little house with land just off State Rd 1 South as you are going to Everton from Connersville about halfway to Everton. The house is located on County Rd 400 S. and the land has a little creek running beside it. The house would be the left side of the road as you travel State Rd 1 South to Everton and is still there as of today. They farmed fruits and vegetables for truck farming which means selling produce from your truck. Truck farming provided a quick income for the family.

The day George and Bertha were married the wedding party and the family went down to Hiram and Sarah's for the reception gathering. This is the house that my mother and father would eat their wedding supper.

It would be only a few months later that George would want to return to Canada. Bertha knew he wanted to go back to the land where Uncle Frank and Aunt Elsie still lived.

4

Homestead in Canada

✦

Summer 1920–1923

Bertha was about 25 years old when George took her back with him to Canada. They would go by way of train staying overnight in a hotel in Winnipeg, Canada and then on by train to Wadena, Saskatchewan, Canada, 400 miles northwest of Winnipeg.

George had left his homestead plot now almost four years ago since he remembered the Indian Chief and his daughter incident. I asked my cousin John Russell Lamb (who was born in Canada) the son of Uncle Frank and Aunt Elsie what he thought George might have done with the livestock that he had on his homestead while he had gone back to Indiana to find a wife. Russell said he didn't know what exactly George would have done with the livestock other than sold them or maybe gave them to his neighbor to take care of. We really don't know who would have taken care of daddy's Canadian homestead while he was gone.

George was returning with a new wife to a log home that he had improved from a shack to a little square house. He had made some furniture; the iron stove and water were all ready in the center of the house. It must have seemed a long way for a small town girl such as Bertha. Mother talked very little about her time in Canada. For the most part she didn't discuss it.

Within the first year of marriage Bertha was pregnant with their first child. He was born on January 15, 1921 and was given the name Albert Ranold Britton. Bertha didn't feel she could have a baby in Canada. Aunt Elsie and her 3 children along with Bertha in the fall of 1920 set out to go back home to Connersville. Hiram, Sarah and Grace had never seen Elsie's two son's John Russell and Frank Gilbert. This was the first trip back that Elsie had made since they had gone up to Canada years earlier. The women with the children rode the train back to Connersville. Bertha rested easier to know that she would give birth in her hometown and not in the Canadian Wilderness.

Albert was born at the home of Bertha's sister, Rosa (Clark) Beck at 2318 Western Avenue in Connersville. We're not sure just how and when George got the message that a son had been born back in Indiana since he was still on the homestead. Home mail delivery just wasn't possible there and is still not available in remote areas today. We feel that Dad must have received word by mail in which he most likely had to pick up in Kelvington.

Elsie and Bertha and the children returned to Canada most likely in the early spring or summer. Bertha didn't have too many friends in Canada, except a young woman about her age that lived not to far from them; this picture shows Bertha with Albert and the neighbor friend with her child.

Bertha Britton & Albert and Friend—1921

George and Bertha now with a young son would survive by simple means. Food would be raised by gardening and farm animals would supply many needs. Daddy used what farm equipment he had to put in his crops; we don't know what they were. Wheat is the most planted crop now with giant granaries in every small town. Life for most young mothers would be just to manage the care of her children. The land and nature must have been beautiful in the early 1920's. Spring and summer would come out for a brief period of heavenly vegetation and the bounty of the food but within just a few months the window of warmth would close and the coldest weather of the land would return.

One day Daddy came in from the land and loosened his horses to trot into the barn lot. Mother looked out the window and saw Albert sitting in the gateway playing. The huge horses with their giant hooves were coming into the passage way right where Albert was. She held her breath with fear. The lead horse stopped and looked at the little guy who was about two years of age. The huge horses begin to walk to the side carefully filing past the young child as he was sitting there playing. Albert was untouched and safe.

Life was difficult in the wilderness of Canada, the winter cold and as mother said the water would freeze before it would hit the ground when she threw it out the door.

When my brother and I drove across the prairie lands on our trip in 1990, we traveled along the same railroad that mother and dad used to arrive in their new home. We got tired and eager to arrive and I began to talk about our trip. I said, "Well, I wonder if Daddy left the land too early, would there be oil there, did he give away our riches?" It's hard to believe our lives would have been better had we all stayed Canadians, though we love our peaceful neighbor to the north. We wouldn't have been given the opportunities in education as we had in the United States and we certainly wouldn't have missed those severe winters.

Daddy must have enjoyed the feeling of family as it shows in this early picture of him and Albert in the year 1921. I'm sure there was enough love to keep them warm that year.

George Britton & Albert 1921

It wasn't long before Bertha was pregnant again this time with Rosie May who would be born May 21, 1922 in Saskatchewan, Canada by a midwife. Elsie had delivered her two sons with help from a Canadian midwife and so Bertha decided she could deliver a baby in Canada, too. After the birth of Rosie that May afternoon, George walked forty miles to report Rosie's birth. When a birth was reported in Saskatchewan the family was given a stipend (extra money) because the country wanted the population to grow. Daddy always said, "Rosie's the only child I had that they paid me to have." All the other children he had to pay for. Bertha told George that their new daughter's name would be May Rose Britton. After George walked the forty miles to report her birth he changed her name to Rosie May Britton. I guess he either forgot what Bertha said or he liked his name for her better.

Families slowly grew in Canada. These are a few more pictures we have added to the Canadian Adventures of the Britton's. The home shown below is Bertha and George's Canadian log home.

Bertha Britton & Rosie May 1922—Canada

George Britton with Rosie & Albert sitting in a chair 1922—Canada

Early the next year, my father would help establish and push for the school that eventually served 25–30 children. This would be the time in which Bertha would become Secretary and Treasurer of the group who was trying to establish the school and Daddy would become the President. As I stated earlier in the story it was thrilling to see the seventy year old documents that were in the actual hand writing of my father and mother during the times they helped to organize a school in Canada. The records had been preserved and kept well by Ida Moss Shirley who Gordon and I had met in 1990 the year we went to Saskatchewan. As you read the minutes of the Board of Trustees it sounds like Bertha was given much of the responsibility of securing supplies, permits, and launching much of the communications process and paying the bills. I can image with two small children the demand this put on her. By summer Bertha was pregnant with her third child when she told the school board that she would be resigning, turning in her books and wanted to return back home in Indiana.

The times in Canada were challenging for many families and it helped to have brothers and sisters close by. Here are Bertha & Elsie's children together in 1922.

Bertha holding Rosie, Ethel holding Albert and Frank Gilbert

Howard Clark, Bertha's brother came to Canada that summer by way of train which he took through North Dakota. He was 21 years old and he told Bertha and George, the train let him off in the middle of the wilderness and the only thing there was the big long cement platform where he was to catch the other train. The conductor told Howard to wait there and that another train would be coming to take him north to Canada. Howard told how alone he felt all by himself there waiting. He hadn't traveled much being a young man. He enjoyed the great outdoors with hunting and shooting the ducks around the lakes.

When Howard was visiting he went out into the yard and found Rosie a year old toddler with her head in the wash tub and her feet sticking up to the sky. Howard reached and snatched her up from the wash water and thus saved her life. It was the summer of 1923.

At the end of Howard's visit, Bertha decided to return back home with Albert and Rosie. They decided it was best for Bertha to travel with Howard. Daddy would need to stay and finish the business of selling the homestead. He had to see to the harvest of the crops at the seasons end. The bank told him they would send him his money back to Indiana. Daddy later would say he didn't get one penny off of the Canadian homestead that he worked so hard to own. George came back to the Britton Egypt Hollow farm of his dad Hiram with absolutely nothing. Stories of his days in Canada would be told to his children throughout his lifetime, but Bertha never really wanted George to tell people about their times in Canada. I guess she remembered them as being stories people wouldn't care to listen to.

Frank and Elsie's family came home to the states with dad in the fall of 1923. Russell Lamb told me at that time the depression was hitting Canada. It would be six years before it would be felt in the United States. Russell said his father, Frank sent cattle via the railroad to the Chicago market and he didn't get enough money for it to pay the passage expenses. When they left their land, they didn't bother to round up the cattle; they were worth nothing and left them on the range.

When you travel through Canada in the Kelvington region and on west to the Rockies you will see little buildings blackened by years of weather and desertion. Evidently many of the early settlers had to give up their dreams and go elsewhere. Today the land is tilled by huge machinery and growing crops that are third in production of the world's food supply. The farm machines have made all this possible. The land is rolling with streams and lakes, lined with trees and birds everywhere around the little lakes. Small churches with huge domes like the top of an onion dot the land; making us know this is Greek Orthodox Country.

Frank continued his occupation in sales and George joined his father in working the land and farming. George and Bertha's family was growing and a new child coming in the next year.

5

Back Home Again in Indiana

✦

1923–1926

When Bertha returned home from Canada she stayed with her two sisters, Ruby and Bessie in their homes which were located on Georgia Avenue in Connersville. They lived next to each other in two small homes that were about 2 blocks from The Central Mgf. Plant. Grace Britton went to town to visit with Bertha and her two small children Albert and Rosie. She was so pleased to see that her brother George had these cute wonderful little happy children.

When daddy returned home from Canada the family stayed with Hiram and Sarah until they would locate to a place of their own. Hiram and Sarah owned a farm they called "Egypt Hollow" in Harmony Township, Union County, Indiana. It was about 88.5 acres. The farm is located on Egypt Hollow Rd. The long lane is still visible from the road. It is a private drive that ends up where the original H.P. Britton house was located along with the farm buildings.

It was here that Willard Gordon Britton was born on January 25, 1924. Dr. Gordin came by way of horse and buggy to deliver the new son of George and Bertha Britton. It was more common to have babies born at home in those days rather than in hospitals like we do today. Gordon was named after Dr. Stanton E. Gordin beloved doctor from Alquina. His first name Willard was for a friend of my mother's from Connersville. Gordon later changed the spelling of his name to Gordon in his early teens.

He was born around the midnight hour. It would be the doctor who would report the birth to the appropriate officials and the birth would be recorded. The Union County Health Department has his name listed as Williard Gordin Britton.

It wasn't long after Gordon's birth when George and Bertha moved just a few miles from Hiram and Sarah to a place called "Shook's Place". The Union

33

County property had a 2 story house. George continued to farm the land and earn a living for his growing family. The "Shook's Place" house has been torn down since our family lived there years ago.

It was the next year that would be remembered as a very sad and emotional time for Bertha and her mother Emma Mae. There was a tuberculosis epidemic outbreak around the area and especially would hit close to home. Tuberculosis is a disease that causes bacteria to grow and attack the lungs and can spread to other parts of the body.

Many people died from the disease.

All in the same year 1925, Bertha would lose her two sisters, Bessie and Ruby to tuberculosis. Bessis died January 1925 leaving three daughters, Charlotte was 11 years old, Audrey was 9 years old and Namoi was 4 years old.

It was on November 17, 1925, that Ruby died leaving one son; Troy Burdette Dawson who we believe was about 10 years of age. Both sisters were married leaving surviving husbands, but the four young children needed more than ever someone to love them like their mother had loved them. Grandmother Emma Mae often watched over the children and gave the loving comfort of a mother.

Bertha took the deaths of her sisters very hard. They had been close and enjoyed wonderful times together. Their children would play together on the sidewalks in town when Ruby and Bessie lived next door to each other. This was another emotional time for Bertha who had just turned twenty-nine years old and now pregnant again.

It was on July 19, 1926 on the "Shooks Place Farm" that I would be born. My mother was in a very poor state of health. She was still hurting and emotionally distressed since the deaths of her sisters. My mother couldn't bear the thought of having another baby and the thoughts of burying her sisters still fresh in her mind. It was a very trying time for my mother. Grandmother Emma came down the day I was born and in fact delivered me. She delivered me before Dr. Gordin came.

Grandmother told me years later that she will go to her grave and she'll never open her mouth as to what happened the day I was born. But I can image my mother said just don't let her breath, but grandmother in her wisdom didn't listen. I was born with the name Lois Cristeen Britton. The doctor said to Emma, "Well you have done all the rest here; you may as well tie the cord." My grandmother cut and tied the cord and I was a living person. Unbeknownst to me when I turned eighteen years old I received a birth certificate listing my name as Lois Cristeen Britton. For as long as I could remember I had always been called Erma Lois. I believe when my mother got better she wanted to change my name to Erma Lois and that's why I was called Erma. My mother's middle name is Emma and o'course my grandmother's name is Emma.

Emma Mae (Fick)

Rosie remembers the day I was born when she was standing on the big porch looking out across the yard and the sun was shinning brightly. The big catalpa trees were in bloom with their cordate leaves and pale showy flowers. She was only four years old when Grandma Emma called for her, "Come here, Rosie I have a surprise for you. You have a baby sister!" And when Rosie looked she saw a tiny little white haired baby laying there in the bed beside her mother she was immediately elated. Rosie remembers being so happy she ran out on the porch and started to sing and dance. All the children were delighted to have a new baby.

I was forty-three years old when I became a grandmother. I decided at that time I would take back part of my name and so I became Grandma Crissie to my grandchildren. Three beautiful little girls; Natalie, Katina, Dana and one bright little boy named Tony.

So the 3rd generation knows me as Grandma Crissie, even my beautiful great grandchildren. I wish our book could tell you all the worthy accomplishments the children in the family line of George and Bertha Britton have brought through their talents. Maybe some day others will contribute their stories of the next generation for them to read. Until then our story continues with the life and times of George and Bertha Britton.

6

From Renting to "Our Place"

✦

1927–1934

From about nine months after my birth our family moved from "Shook's Place" to many other different farms over several years. We mostly lived around the Rush County, Indiana area on farm properties my daddy would rent and share crop. He would say that every time he would clean up a farm the owner would decide to sell it and the family would have to move again. We must have moved at least four times in those years.

Grandpa Hiram and Grandma Sarah celebrated their 50th Wedding Anniversary in the summer of 1928. The Britton family gathered at the Egypt Hollow Farm for a family picture and celebration. I was only two years old and sitting on my dad, George's lap. Hiram and Sarah's family had grown since the 1903 family picture taken down in Owenton, Kentucky.

First row left to right; Harold Grimes, Dale Britton, Milton Britton, Gilbert Lamb, Albert Britton, Glenda (Britton) Binder, Rosie (Britton) McKinney, Virginia (Britton) Fischer.
Second row; Nellie (Britton) Grimes, Erma (Britton) Moore, George A. Britton, Hiram & Sarah Britton, Howard Britton, Ollie (Newkirk) Britton, Gordon Britton, Edith (Britton) Wilson, Russell Lamb.
Third row; Roberta (Grimes) Rush, Bertha (Clark) Britton, Marjorie (Britton) Church, Goldie (Britton) Hines, Doris (Britton) McCrory, Ethel (Heath) Britton, Walter Britton.
Fourth row; Robert Grimes, Evelyn (Grimes) Brandenburg, Elsie (Britton) Lamb, Frank Lamb, Dempsey Britton, Charles Britton, Grace Britton, Florence (Grimes) Tyra, Ethel (Lamb) Seaney.

Albert entered the first grade in New Salem when we lived on "Shook's Place", and in the middle of his first grade we moved to a place called "Springers" which was located in the Rushville, Indiana area. He completed his first year of grade school in Glenwood, Indiana. Rosie's first year in school was in Glenwood, too.

We were very poor and just didn't have much. Rosie remembers learning about Halloween in the first years of school. She had never heard of such a day. Rosie returned home from school and told mother she had to wear a mask to school for Halloween. Mother took a green cloth and cut out a square rag with eyes and gave her a hat to wear and put powder around Rosie's head. That was her Halloween costume. When Rosie got to school the other children all had fancy costumes and she just got out her mask and was ready for the parade. The children ate popcorn and had fun. Rosie's teacher liked having her in the first grade because Rosie could help the slow learners.

The places around Rushville we rented ranged from a very small little country house to a beautiful farm mansion around the Harrisburg area. Leta Risk owned the mansion that had been built during the Civil War. The Risk house was located 2.5 miles west of Harrisburg on road 400N in Fayette County.

We were excited to move into the big house. The square house had an open circular staircase that went to a third floor where there was a great big room like a ballroom. Rosie my sister said she remembers playing upstairs in that big room. There was a play area that had a little kitchen set with toys, dolls and everything children would love to play with We got to live there about 2 years. Rosie and Albert attended Harrisburg School when we lived on the Risk farm. Albert was eight, Rosie was seven, Gordon was five and I was 3 years old. My mother was so happy when we lived there. I believe if we could have always lived there her life would have seemed so complete. Again the Risk farm mansion was for sale and we had to move.

My father's first car was a Star sedan. Our family acquired the car during the time we lived at the Risk farm. Riley Clark who was our great uncle owned the Star car. He had driven his family to California so the car had earned a reputation of being a reliable car. You know how everyone is about their first car so we choose to include this in our story. There were only three Star automobiles lines made in a short time period during the middle 1920's.

My father had a chance to buy a farm and it would be the only farm he would ever own. It was a farm located along Bear Creek 2 miles southwest of Everton, Indiana in Jackson Twp., on Little Bear Road. The farm was 88 ½ acres with nice fertile land for raising crops, virgin forest with a wealth of trees and Bear Creek ran thought the farm. We would harvest the nuts from the trees and make candy with delicious fresh nuts.

Daddy bought the farm on Bear Creek October 9, 1929. You can image how my father must have felt. Now with land he could own and wouldn't have to worry about the owners selling after he had worked so hard to make improvements. He bought the farm through the Fayette Bank & Trust Company in Connersville.

The property had a log cabin. The cabin was situated across the road from the creek and before it stood four huge pine trees. Our front lawn was rolling green land and a stone laid front patio. We closed the main front door and opened an eastern door that lead to a large room. This room was used for a sitting room, music room, a library, and a bedroom. Daddy built a six foot long, five shelf bookcase on one wall.

Inside the cabin was a fireplace we didn't use but instead used a little tin stove for warmth in the big room. There was a built-in wardrobe and a curved stairway that lead up to the attic. The chimney came up through the attic and there was a window where you could look outside. It was a favorite place for young children especially during inclement weather where we could stay warm by the chimney. Albert and Gordon slept in the attic even thought it was not a finished room and you could see daylight at the line of the eves.

Marshall Kirk, Grandma Emma's husband helped daddy build on to the cabin. They added additional living space with a middle room that served like a walkway from the log cabin and new part of house. It was the middle room that was a bedroom for Rosie and me. The new section had a tin roof. When it would rain we kids would like to go and lie on the bed and listen to the rain.

In the attic was a trunk of questionable vintage in which mother had stored all the fine things from former days. There was a little white flannel coat with scalloped cape collar that my brother Albert had worn, and a long braid of dark brown hair from the day my mother cut off her long hair. There were many other things in this trunk and we often played dress-ups. Why she let us do this I'll never know as this trunk contained valuables like my father's love letters to my mother. How I would love to have those now. Things that are precious and sacred should be kept for the new generation until they can really appreciate their value.

I was still a pre-schooler when we moved to Bear Creek. I had much time to build dream castles and fictional friends. When we drove to Connersville for shopping my little heart would soar within my bosom in anticipation. Our home was quiet, no radio, no phone and only a daily paper but it was soon to become the focal point of the day after our noon meal. Everyone would get a section they wanted to read and the paper would be completed separated.

Being the youngest of four children, I enjoyed a special relationship with my father, who after the close of a long working day in the fields would sit before the fire resting and holding me on his lap, many times telling us stories, sometimes so sad that we would break out crying, and mother would say, "George, now don't tell those sad tales." If only my father would have written down these stories and all the wonderful things that filled his mind, we children could have known fame and fortune.

Here's my sketched drawing of the Bear Creek Farm. EBM-2004

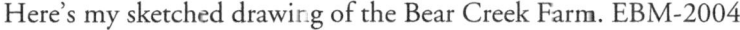

We had many wonderful times on the Bear Creek farm. It was our own and a real farm!

In the late twenties, the economic situation in the country had improved and for the first time my folks could buy a few of the nicer things, included was a black silk coat trimmed with fringe of horse hair and a elegant gray chiffon dress trimmed with gold medal medallions for mother. My father had a new suit.

We went to Everton School and rode the bus to school. Buses were owned by individual people so if the area you lived in was rich you were lucky enough to ride a school bus to school. There were several children in the Everton School who were very intelligent. We all made good grades. The Everton School was small. Some levels of upper class grades were combined so the classroom size was bigger. This allowed for students to earn enough credits to graduate from high school.

Albert and Rosie related more to each other because they were so much closer to each other in age. They competed for grades in school and challenged each other many times. Rosie said growing up in her childhood was bleak. She could never get enough reading materials and read every book in the little Everton School library. She had learned to read before she went to school by Albert bringing home his first grade book.

Rosie could read all the beginner books that Albert brought home from school.

The brilliant children who learned to read would always succeed regardless of their circumstances. Rosie worked in the library at the Everton School. Her classroom was next to the school's library and when a student wanted to check out a book she would leave her desk and go to the library to check out the book.

At our home on Bear Creek we only had a few books to read. I remember the Autobiography of Abraham Lincoln, "The Journey from the Log Cabin to the White House." Well at the time we all felt that our story was entitled, "The Journey from the White House to the Log Cabin." since we had lived in the big Civil War home in the Harrisburg area. Dad had several books that a lady had given him. I was too young to read but remember some graphic pictures in a World War I book showing emaciated forms of human beings caused by the role of the Turks and how they let the people starve.

We had some fun times playing along the creek in the sand and water. We would build sandcastles and pretend to plant our garden. Berries would be coffee, weeds would be celery, rocks would be eggs and this would be our created play. There were pigs and chickens and an aggressive old rooster who would run us back into the yard when we would go out to bring in the wood. There was a ravine with a big grapevine to swing out and across and the barn to play in the rafters on new hay. It was quiet living in the country. Nothing much ever permeated the stillness, so creating an echo from the wooded land across the creek was fine play.

Mother taught Albert and Rosie how to read music and play simple songs on an old "pump" organ we owned. Bertha never thought she could play well enough for church but she could play the melody of some hymns.

We had cows and milked them and saved the cream. We sold the cream as it was another cash crop. Mother made butter packaged with a butter pat flower which made it look very nice to sell. Dad would go to town and sell our produce. He would buy groceries, coal oil for our lamps and gasoline for the car. When George would go to town usually on Saturdays, mother would say to Rosie, "now get ready and go to town with dad. He will take you up to Ruby's house." Ruby was our preachers red haired beautiful daughter who taught Rosie the basics of piano. Dad would drop her off when he took his produce to sell in town. Her music lesson cost 35 cents. This was a real sacrifice dad would make for Rosie to learn to play music, for 35 cents would have helped to repair the old harness for his horses and many other things he needed for farming. Mother insisted that Rosie have music lessons It was Bertha that encouraged Rosie to develop her musical talents we all enjoy still today.

Our family attended the Nazarene Church which was located on West Fourth Street in Connersville. There were many families with children who we met in the Sunday school classes. We enjoyed Sundays. It was a day to rest and visit with our wonderful church friends. Sometimes during the harsh Indiana winter days we couldn't make the trip to town for church services, so we gathered to worship in our own home. We enjoyed singing all together, playing our music, daddy teaching us Bible lessons and all kneeling down to pray.

Albert and Gordon learned how to set and run trap lines on the Bear Creek farm.

Albert told me he would catch skunks maybe a muskrat. He said Gordon caught some nice fox. Gordon was upset when mother bought Albert the first new bike. She used the money from trapping to purchase it. Later in the story you will read that Gordon got the first car.

Our daily newspaper The Richmond Palladium Item was delivered in the mail. Rosie liked to keep things and gathered many items. In the paper there was a picture of a dress you could send off for the pattern. These were of dresses you could sew for yourself. You had to order the pattern by mail. Rosie would cut the picture of the dress out of the newspaper and used them for her paper dolls. She had two paper dolls named Katie Benfulls & Christeen. At one point she had 400 dresses for her dolls.

She would lay the dresses out across the pillows on her bed to make a wardrobe. Then she would decide and plan what the paper doll girls would do for the day or the outing. She would dress them in different dresses and sometimes I would play with them, too. Albert would sometimes sneak into her room and blow all the paper dresses all over the room.

When you have several siblings in the family sometimes we get the feeling that some get more attention than others. I guess we are all like that at times. Mother seemed to favor Albert and Rosie. Daddy seemed to favor Gordon and me. I was the baby of the family during this time period. I was bright and very happy. I remember just bouncing happily around in the yard.

The bottom land of the Bear Creek farm was a sandy soil composite and daddy found out he couldn't grow corn very well there. He was skilled in farming and knew he could raise some mighty big watermelons in that area. The melons he produced proved he was right. I'm not joking some of the melons were 3 feet long.

One summer he planned on entering his prize watermelon in the Fayette County Free Fair. You see the neighbor boys liked to raid the watermelon patch in the night, so the morning dad went down to pick his prize winner melon it was gone. Dad did pick his second biggest melon and took it to the fair that day. When he got there he found his 3 ft long prize winner watermelon laying on the table with another man's name from Everton on it. So dad got second prize and the other man got first.

We had two big horses dad used to work on the farm. Madge was a big dapple gray horse and Ole Bob a big red horse that was just starting in his prime for working and was only 8 years old. He was so big and strong. They made a great team. One day Gordon and I went to play near by the creek that was down in the horse pasture. I told Gordon that I knew where there were some apples. Dad had always warned us about staying away from the horses and not to play in the pasture.

We didn't listen to him that day. I was 4 years old and Gordon was 6 years old at this time. It was a Saturday morning in September and dad was helping a man cut wood and wasn't home at the time. I had to climb over a gate which was about 6 or 7 ft high. It was used to keep the horses inside the pasture area. Ole Bob and Madge were there close by us as I started to climb over the gate. I was just about over the gate when I thought I better tell Gordon to be quiet not to upset the horses. He liked to watch the horses run and at that moment he clapped his hands to make the horses run and the big huge thrust of Madge's hoof hit the gate.

The force threw me about 25 or 30 feet down by the creek. I hit the ground and remembered looking up at the sky and Gordon running down and I said to him, "Don't touch me just go get mom." So he ran back to the house which wasn't very far. Mom said when she looked at his little face he couldn't say a word and just pointed to the creek. The next thing I remembered was mom carrying me to house with a pillow under my leg. My leg looked as big as a balloon. Mother laid me on her bed in the log cabin. It was warm in there. Albert was there, too. Daddy came home and they called the doctor. I remember looking out the door and seeing Gordon's sad little face looking in at me.

The trip to the hospital I vaguely recall. I had broken the femur in my left leg. Dr. Morrow who was the best surgeon at the hospital came to look at my leg. Daddy said to him, "I don't have much money but I have chickens I can pay you with." The doctor said to him, "She's young and she needs a good leg." They stretched my leg and set it in a leg cast. My grandmother Emma stayed with me in the hospital and she said ever once in awhile I would scream out. I stayed in the hospital for a few days and then went to grandma house. Later I returned back home. One day after I had returned home with my leg still in the cast mom saw Bob our big red horse out standing by the gate. He stood there for sometime and mom said it was like Ole Bob wanted to see me. Mom picked me up and carried me to the window. Later mom said Ole Bob never came back to the gate again.

The doctor came to our house six weeks later to cut off the cast. I remember seeing my leg all wrinkled and I wanted him to put the cast back on. I had to learn to walk again all over. I walked with a limp for a short while because I had lost about an inch in the bone. The only adjustment I have to make today is a one inch adjusted hem line on my skirts.

One spring on Bear Creek Farm, my brother Albert recalled a story of how daddy was too sick to work on the farm. He had been suffering from sinus headaches and just didn't feel well enough to even begin work on the farm. It was early in the spring and the farm land needed tilled so the corn could be planted. The season was rapidly approaching and much work was still to be completed. Dale Britton, our first cousin who was a few years older than we were, came to help us that year. He came and plowed and disked the land. Albert helped him and they planted the corn.

In the process of working over the 400 ft circle of dirt that we planted in corn, Dale suddenly realized he had lost his brand new knife. He was quite disappointed after he looked hopelessly across the freshly plowed dirt. "How am I ever going to find my brand new knife," he said to Albert.

Albert in deep thought answered and said to him, "Where do you think it might be?" After looking at the expression Dale gave him Albert knew this was a needle in the haystack. He knew that God could help him find Dale's knife, but how in the world could he do it? Albert started walking in a big circle with faith and believing with every step that God would help him to find Dale's knife. He walked around and suddenly he stopped as if this was where God wanted him to stop. Then Albert felt like he should dig a hole and under six inches of dirt the brand new knife appeared in as fine as shape as if it were just out of Dale's pocket.

Dale Britton was one our favorite cousins and now many years later he has gone on to be with the Lord. Albert wrote him a letter several months before his passing and talked about how God can help us through many times in our lives. He recalled the story of the brand new knife and how God had answered prayer for Dale that day many years ago down on a farm. Albert told of how he gave his life to Jesus and how Dale too could believe and have assurance that God will see him through everything life would bring his way.

Mother worked hard on the Bear Creek farm. She would shuck corn, keep up the housework, canned our food, and baked the best homemade bread and huge big biscuits. She raised the baby chickens and in the springtime mother would get the incubators ready. These were about forty inch square drawers made out of galvanized material with a little lamp on the side which stayed lit all the time and kept the eggs warm until they hatched. Each day mother would turn the eggs; I guess that each tray would take about a hundred eggs. It was wonderful to see them hatch. A thermometer lay inside the tray on the eggs to tell her whether the temperature was right. Later mother began to buy the chicks from a commercial hatchery and the mailman would bring a big box full of baby chicks a couple times each spring.

It was always fun when dad would load up the car with corn and take it to our neighbor, Mr. Scott to get it ground into chicken feed. Usually he would pile the car so full there wasn't room for us. Gordon and I would stand on the road head hung sideways watching the car disappear down the road wishing we could have gone along.

Another time of great interest was during sorghum making; and once we made it at our place. Many people came to help and a huge big wooden tub under which a fire was built was filled with the sap that had been wrung from the stalks of the sugar cane. Then a big stir stick was fastened into the middle of the vat and in turn was fastened to a lead line which the horses would walk around the circle and thus stirred the boiling mixture until it became thick and like syrup. The mixture had to be skimmed off and that part thrown away from time to time. It was a big job and more times than not dad would take his cane over to Mr. Ruff's place to have the sorghum made. Sorghum was sharp tasting syrup which no one liked too well, but it was better than nothing on our pancakes and mush. Dad liked it the best. Ha!

Butchering was another task most farmers did each winter. We didn't butcher very much. Usually Grandpa Hiram would be butchering and he would do one or two hogs for us. We usually were too poor to spare many of the hogs for our own use. Many of our neighbors butchered beef but we never had a beef cow to butcher.

Fall was a time of making catsup and cold packing the green beans. Mother's sister and her mother would come down from town to help. They would build the fire outside and can in big copper boilers. It would take all day to cook the tomatoes down to make catsup with the right consistency. There was much work to do on the farm. Farming afforded us a fair living with some to give away to those who were poorer than we were.

We had a little horse that was too small to work in the field. Daddy would let us ride her. One poor neighbor had no horse. Dad lent our small horse to him to put in his garden produce for his truck farming. We later learned he let our little horse starve. There were rumors around our neighborhood that some poor people would lose a child at birth and just bury it rather than have a public burial because of the expense. Poor people have poor ways.

Around our neighborhood almost every family lost at least one child through disease or accident. Mother was always so thankful that this never happened to us. We had no fires and no bad illnesses. Surely God was looking out for us.

Daddy conducted some church services at The Stone Chapel Church in Franklin County, Indiana which was about 5 or 6 miles from our Bear Creek farm. The farm community was really poor with very few cars. I remember seeing the people walking down the red soil dirt roads to come to church. Some people would ride their horses and tie them to the trees outside the church. They would pack the church. I remember thinking this must be what it would look like if you were working as a missionary in the mission fields and witnessing the local needy people walking to church. The people didn't have money for much entertainment and going to church gave them an opportunity to get out and do something. Dad preached for several years on Sunday afternoons and they were good and happy times. Then the depression hit.

7

The Great Depression

✦

1934–Spring 1937

The depression really came about 1929 but didn't hit the agricultural regions until about 1933. The prices on the crops were dropping. Bad times came in many events and one was the story of our big beautiful gray horse Madge. Somehow Madge got a rusty nail in her foot. The veterinarian came but there was nothing he could do for Madge and she died of lockjaw. After that we only had our big red horse Bob. This was tragic for George because he knew you just can't farm with only one horse.

Grandpa Hiram brought his team of mules ten miles to help dad put in the corn that year. Everyone including us children hand picked the harvest at the end of the corn season. Dad realized he had no choice but to sell our loved horse Ole Bob. I'm sure my father would have rather done most anything else.

He bought two plug horses. The lead horse was a big brown horse we called "Dick" and "Dolly" was a little fat blind horse that could only follow the lead horse. She worked well with Dick. We were always afraid that Dolly might get out of the barn lot and fall down the ravine to the creek. It had washed some and was now about twelve feet just below the road. When the creek would flood the water would fill to the top and run over the road. We were taught to respect things of nature and one of them was the creek at flood time. Sure enough one day Dolly got out of the barn lot and wandered up in front of the house on the road. There she was just ready to fall over the ravine. We all yelled I think or maybe we all just froze in silence and watched Dolly put out the next great hoof into the nothingness above the creek. All the sudden she stopped and turned and we all breathed easily now that she was safe.

Daddy planted the crops that year with his new team, but prices were continuing to fall and the depression was really taking hold. One by one, the hogs, the cows and the horses were sold. It was the summer of 1934 and daddy couldn't make enough money on his corn. He couldn't keep up the payments on the Bear Creek farm causing a foreclosure. Gordon remembers dad telling him that he got 6 cents a pound for hogs, 8 cents a bushel for corn, and 10 cent a dozen for eggs, you just couldn't make it with those prices.

One day an employee of the Fayette Bank who no doubt worked in the loan department came down to our farm. He was out on a mission to take back our farm. My dad wasn't even home at the time. Mother was pregnant and the hateful man hollered in a very mean tone of voice to her and ordered us to be off the farm within 30 days of the 1st of March. Gordon was upstairs looking out the window watching and heard the bad-tempered angry man speaking loud to mother. He said it was all he could do not to pick up a brick that was laying upstairs by the chimney and throw it out the window on the man's head.

My dad was very, very angry when he returned from the field and heard the story of how the man from the bank came down and talked mean to Bertha. He went to the bank and protested and told them what had happened and the bank apologized with all they had. It didn't change anything. We lost the farm and had to move on again.

We rented a little black house the next year on Big Bear Road that lead to Nulltown. It was a three room house and rented for $3.00 per week. Across the road was a little red brick four room house that had previously been a schoolhouse. Our wonderful neighbors were Alma and Bob Bowman. They were from the Cincinnati area. They didn't have any children. Bob was a salesman who made his living working on the road and wasn't home to often. Alma became a very good friend of my mother's. Alma just loved Gordon. He was a very cute shy little boy. Often times in the depression people would offer to take children in families where there were many children to raise. It was hard for many to have enough to even feed the family. Gordon was the child that people would say to mother, "let me take your Gordon." Mother would say, "I'd never give one of my children away."

The place had a barn that we could keep a cow, a garden, a wash room outside and a chicken house. I say the little house was black because most of the paint had peeled and flaked off. The house was in great need. It had two rooms with a big long kitchen on the back. Out back was a shed mother used for a washroom. Daddy stored firewood in the shed, too. We had a barn in which we kept the cow. The farm land surrounding the little house was farmed out to other neighbors.

These were tough times through the depression but we always had food to eat. Mother was a good cook and we raised good food on the land. We didn't have all the things other children had. Mother cooked our lunches and wrapped them in newspapers and used a straight pin to close it. The other children at school would make fun at us when we brought our newspaper wrapped lunches. We never felt real comfortable with some of the children we went to school with because of the things they would say about us being poor.

Dad was very sad that he had lost his beloved farm on Bear Creek the one farm he could say was his own. He had to farm himself out for day labor making $2.00 per day and work for other people. He said he needed to do something more and decided to take a line of products and go door to door selling as many people did during those times.

He told the family he was taking some Bibles and offered them for sale on his route.

You know, the Lord blessed his efforts and he sold far more Bibles than the products he offered.

Mother was going to have another baby that summer and she didn't tell us children early on. The spring was cold and bitter and my father suffered from headaches from having to work outside in the raw cold weather. He was sad and ill. Mother prayed that he would live to see the child she was carrying grow up. She must have been really worried about my father during this time. School occupied the time for us children and there were neighbor children to play with. Sometimes I think my mother must have been the loneliest of all of us. The winter turned into spring and soon the summertime.

The first year Connersville had fireworks was in the summer of 1935. My mother's brothers, Howard and Elmer, often times visited us in the county. You could hear them coming in their cars since the country was so quite. They loved seeing and being with us children. One day they came to visit and told mother and dad they should take us children to Connersville because the town was celebrating the Fourth of July with a big fireworks display. We did go and it was wonderful to see the fireworks at the Roberts Park. It still is today one of the best showing of fireworks around the State of Indiana.

It was in this house that George and Bertha's last child Sarah Judith Britton was born on August 5, 1935. Judy was a frail and beautiful little child. She brought much joy and happiness to all of our family. Rosie especially was very fond of this little new baby we had. She would take care of her and we all loved her very much.

When the crops came that fall daddy worked for other farmers around the area. We raised a garden that year and if we had any produce daddy would go to town and sell his produce. Mr. Sykes who owned the A & P Store on 16th Street in Connersville bought from daddy and Mr. Sykes would give him all the bread that didn't sell because not many people had the money to buy. He figured that dad could feed the chickens with the bread. We had the finest bread ever.

Mother quit making bread because we had all the bread we ever needed. One evening a neighbor girl told us they had to go to town to get bread. I said to her, "You don't have to do that we have a whole basket full of bread just take a loaf with you."

We lived in the little black rented house for nine months. Our luck was about to change. Times were hard, but little did we know how lucky we were to have each other. Our family would be complete now; George and Bertha with their children, Albert 14, Rosie 13, Gordon 11, Erma 9 and Judy a newborn baby. Mother and dad loved each other very much. Dad was always a perfect gentleman. Even though his affections for mother were hardly visibly expressed, his love for her was constant. I can't say it enough the most wonderful part of our family was the love we expressed for each other.

◆   ◆   ◆

Grandpa Hiram owned two farms during the time of the depression; one on Duck Creek and the Egypt Hollow farm. Grandpa Hiram farmed the land on both properties. He lived on Egypt Hollow and rented the two story house on the Duck Creek farm. This house was located on 750S about 2 miles southeast of Everton. If you try and find the little house today you won't, but you will see the little creek that runs through the Duck Creek farm which is located on the Southside of 750S.

Hiram gave notice to the renters that they would need to leave because his son, George and his family was in need of the house. It was a nice house we knew because daddy's brother Howard had built it several years earlier. The house was very adequate for our family. Aunt Grace kept the varnished mahogany woodwork nicely polished. It had 2 little rooms upstairs that we just loved. The boys got one bedroom and the girls got the other. They had windows you could look outside. Mom and dad's bedroom was downstairs. We moved into the house in the wintertime. We all loved this place and once again we felt like we were living.

We had no crop and no money. George got a loan from the land bank (National Farm Recovery Act) to start farming again. He borrowed $500 for starting up the farm. Mother had to keep a farm record of all income and expenses. Every several weeks a lady from the government office would come and check my mother's books. We had to pay back the loan at $100 per year plus interest when the crops would be harvested.

Daddy bought two horses and everything he needed to start farming. One of the horses we called "Big White Charlie" was huge and very strong and the other was black and called "Dolly".

It was a really cold winter that year with temperatures 22 below zero degrees. It was the coldest winter on record, a terribly cold winter. We didn't miss much school and the buses ran regularly. Albert would ride his bike about 3/4 mile to the east on 750S to the McKoaun's farm and bring home a pint of milk from their Jersey heifer. Mother always said, "the younger the cow the better the milk." She wanted the best for her young daughter, Judy. Albert would come home from riding his bike there and his face would be covered with big red blotches from the freezing air.

We really had very little. My mother's brother Howard brought some shoes for my sister. Mother began to show the signs of strain and would keep me home too long doing morning work causing me to miss the bus which came out in front of our block long lane. My feet would freeze because I had holes in my shoe soles and I would cry on arriving at school. One of the boys felt sorry for me and took me to the furnace room to warm my feet. My mother found out and thought I was doing something bad down there and she whipped me. She seemed incensed with the idea that we were going to do something bad, all of us kids.

Christmas at school was a happy time for us. We received treats from the teachers and a generous treat from the bus driver and a special program at school. That year I had a very special part. Once again my mother kept me working at home too late to catch the bus and I missed it on this special day. I just would not miss this special time at school and I sat out to walk the three miles or so to school. The sun though bright could not dispel the cold wind that rushed through my thin coat, but on I plodded. Our rich neighbor Mrs. Kellum who was a young bride came along in her big warm late model car and asked me where I was going. I said, "to school" and she took me all the way there. Someday I want to tell this lady how much that ride meant to me.

We just didn't have any money for Christmas that year. Gordon and Albert had gone into the woods in the trapping season to check the lines for their catches. It was three days before Christmas and Albert went out to run the traps and found a muskrat caught in his trap. He took the muskrat on the school bus to Everton where there was a taxidermist. The man took the muskrat and paid

Albert $3.00 for his hide. Albert took the money home to his mother and she went to town and bought every one of us a Christmas present and we had a little tree with fancy little bulbs she had gotten from Aunt Ruby. We had no Christmas lights, no electricity, no radio, but we always had a fresh cut hillside cedar evergreen. The Lord saw fit for us to have a special Christmas that year and the little muskrat in the trap was a blessing.

Rosie learned to play classical music from Mr. Sholl. The Everton School had hired him as their new music teacher. Mr. Sholl came to our house in the summer where Rosie would learn to play more piano music. Daddy often went around and preached at churches that didn't have a pastor. It was about this time that Rosie played her first song at a church. She was only thirteen and dad wanted her to play for the service. She played three songs on a pump organ. The next time she would have learned three more songs so her musical talents began to flourish.

The summers were mostly uneventful but the summer of 1937 we had a real scare with our little Judy. She was two years old when she began to have problems with loosing her breath. They never knew exactly why she did this other than the statement that Judy was a frail fragile little child. It was a summer day. Mother was doing hand washing with a big round tub of rinse water outside. I was with Judy in the kitchen when she lost her breath. We were always told that when she would do this we would get some cold water and splash her face with it. This would normally bring her breath and she would be OK. So I took her to the pitcher pump which was in the kitchen (water we used for laundry and washing). I doused her forehead and tried to get her to come to but it didn't work. It was then when I took her out to mother.

Mom tried to get her to come to and couldn't bring her back. Daddy was in the vegetable garden which was down over a hill and across a pasture. Almost about two blocks from the house. Mother carried Judy in the backyard next to the wood shed. We called for daddy to come up and help us. He heard our call and began to walk.

Daddy continued to walk and we thought he should be running. But he didn't he just continued to walk up the hill. There was a spring down there in the valley next to the creek. When daddy got up the hill, mother laid the little limp body of Judy in his arms. We kids were in the yard at this time screaming to God to bring our baby back. Daddy laid Judy's body on his big long arms. He stretched out his big strong arms and he rolled her down his arms and in bringing her back and forth he blew a big puff of air into her mouth. The air being the air he had saved from walking up the hill. After a few big puffs we heard a little sigh of life. He brought her back to life and she began to breath. Daddy never went back to the garden that day. That was the worst attack of loosing her breath she ever had. She continued on and off to experience these breathing problems until she was about five years old.

Bless the Lord; our first harvest of crop had come in on the Duck Creek Farm! This made us all very happy. Prices were going up and the country was recovering from the depression. We had an abundance of crops in the harvest enough that mom sent Albert down to God's Bible School in Cincinnati to study the Bible and go to divinity school. He was still in high school but could get credits there, too. She wanted him to become a minister. Albert didn't really have much, not very many clothes, but he did have a really sharp brain.

The students from God's Bible School came up to our farm in a big truck one day.

They were kids who were poor, and worked hard to go to school and wanted to come and visit the farm. There were about six of them in the group. Daddy filled up their truck with beans, pumpkins, squash, tomatoes, all the vegetables that the last September garden would produce. Mother fixed the boys a big meal and they ate fried chicken in our kitchen. Albert returned with them to start school.

Albert was learning new technologies and gaining knowledge. He was studying the Bible and increasing his interest in electronics and the world around him. Albert read all about radios and how to build crystal sets and loved listening to the radio. He would stay up all night listening to the radio. He eventually decided he wanted a career in electronics and that's what he wanted to do in his life.

I remember riding the bus to school the year that Albert had gone down to God's Bible School. The kids on the bus talked and said, "Let it be known that Albert Britton is going to be a preacher." When the bus passed Hiram Pierce Britton's mailbox and on the mailbox was H.P. Britton. The kids would say, "There's *High Power* Britton's house." Anyway that's the kind of things kids would say on the school bus.

My mother seemed happier now. She studied intently the world situation and talked a lot to my Grandfather Hiram about the unions and the world situations. I remember hearing about war for the first time that year. I was 10 years old and Ethiopia was being invaded. Little did I know then that was the beginning of the rest of my life where I would always be aware of a war someplace in the world.

In January 1937 the big flood came in Cincinnati and Newport clear up into the towns. The Ohio River runs through Cincinnati, Ohio and Newport, Kentucky which is across the river from Cincinnati. Nearly one of every eight people in the Tri-State was left homeless. Almost one-fifth of Cincinnati was covered by water. Seven months before the flood, President Franklin D. Roosevelt had signed legislation ordering the U.S. Army Corps of Engineers to begin constructing flood protection for the Ohio and other major rivers. The '37 flood sped up that effort.[7]

My dad's brother, Walter, lived in Newport with his family and they had to move all their furniture to the 2nd floor of their home. The flood waters came in all the homes on the first floors in the whole town of Newport. Albert helped to move furniture and many of the young boys who were attending God's Bible School were sent out by the school in boats to rescue people who were stranded in the flood waters. Mother always said later that she would have never wanted her son to go out into the dangers of fast river waters and she commented that she hadn't sent her boy down there to drown. She was very concerned for Albert's safety.

Albert only stayed at God's Bible School one year. He had become increasing more interested in electronics than the possibility of being a preacher. He wanted to continue learning more about the radio. He lost so much sleep listening to the radio at night that in May the school called and told mom and dad that they needed to come and get Albert. He was having hallucinations because of sleep deprivation. They said he needed to go home and rest. He never went back to divinity school.

◆   ◆   ◆

Grandfather Hiram at 77 years old was ready to quit and retire from the rigors of farming and so the Egypt Hollow Farm was sold May 6, 1937 to Kenneth R. Graham and the Duck Creek Farm sold, too. Both farms now had been sold and the family gathered the funds and Grandfather Hiram and Grandmother Sarah decided to retire. We had enjoyed living on the Duck Creek Farm for about two years. Mr. Graham offered my father the chance to move over to the Egypt Hollow Farm and so we did.

◆   ◆   ◆

There was a terrible tragedy in the fall of 1937. Walter Britton my dad's brother had started and was running a coal business in Newport, Kentucky. A new driver was operating the coal truck when he accidentally backed the truck into Walter. The truck crushed Walter into the wall of the building and he lost his life that day in the tragic accident. He was a young, strong six foot man of 39 years old who left a wife named Ethel with four young little girls. The youngest was about 9 months old and the oldest being in her early teens. Our family went down to Newport for the funeral. It was a very sad time.

The next year Dempsey, dad's other brother and also brother of Walter, went down to Newport to help Ethel the widow of Walter, with the coal business. Dempsey knew that he had to help during this difficult time in Ethel's life. Dempsey himself had lost a wife Ava Juanita (Trusler) who died September 12, 1924. At the time of his wife's death they had three living children. Dempsey and his children had been living with Hiram and Sarah helping out on the farm. Later Ethel and Dempsey were married. In their retirement, Ethel and Dempsey spent about twenty-five years in Florida until their deaths.

Walter Britton, a cousin, Grace Britton and George Britton
1919 Newport, Kentucky

This picture shows the young single Brittons with an unidentified cousin.

8

Life on "Egypt Hollow"

❖

Fall 1937–1940

After daddy decided to accept Mr. Graham's offer we rented the Egypt Hollow Farm. This had been the Land of his father; and now the Land of Ours. Looking over the fields today takes us back in our minds to a time when we all gathered and enjoyed our families.

This was like going home again for George to the place where he had brought Bertha back from Canada, now with his own family. He would plow the fields, plant the seeds and harvest the crop on the land his father had loved; a farm he had grown to respect and a time he would enjoy his own family.

We moved over to the home place farm and lived there for the next five years. Farm prices were going up and we were on the fertile land of the original Britton homestead. Once again farming was good. The farm house at Egypt Hollow was about a half mile off the main road. We would have to walk down a long lane which was our driveway to meet the school bus. The house was too small for us children and we still had no radio or electricity.

The elementary school was located at Dunlapsville and offered grades one through eight. It was a new school and offered a free hot lunch program. My brother Gordon and I attended there and I was just finishing the sixth grade at that time. My sister Judy would later attend first grade and a part of second. We really liked the school even though we had to ride the bus two hours each day. This was the first time I had some academic competition. The people were fairly well off and one nice lady gave me a bag of nice dresses and clothes, including a wool cape suit. I was beginning to feel happy for the first time in my life.

Albert and Rosie had to transfer from Everton School to Alquina School which provided the High School grades ninth through twelfth. Our family still didn't have much money. The government set up different programs and organizations to help support the youth in the communities. Albert and Rosie signed up for the NYA (National Youth Administration) which provided part-time employment for students to earn $6.00 per month. Albert worked his senior year for the Alquina School doing Janitor work. He could get his homework done quickly and he worked about 20 hours per week. Rosie worked at the school, too. She did administration work such as typing tests and office work. She learned her typing and shorthand at the Alquina School. This was a good deal for them since it provided extra income to help buy their clothes and items they might not have had otherwise.

Rosie and Albert both finished their high school years at Alquina. They still occasionally return to enjoy their class reunions.

The children in our family were wonderful children who were bright and fun loving. We attended school regularly and were all at the top of our classes. Years later we would hear some of our classmates say how they tried to beat the Britton's on the tests and never could beat them.

Daddy many times took care of us before we would go to school. He would get us up early to catch the school bus. His breakfast menu would be oatmeal and a wonderful quick bread he would make for us. It was called banic bread made with lots of eggs and was yellow when baked. He had learned to make this bread while he was in Canada. The round loaf prepared with lots of butter would come out of the oven with a high peak and piping hot. Daddy always did a lot for us and was a great force in our lives. He loved to teach us about the Bible and tell stories in the evenings. We loved him very much.

Mom helped dad and worked right beside him but she was never too strong. When she would tuck us children in bed for the night we would talk about the day and pray just before we would go to sleep. She always showed us her love by her gentle spirit. Often the next morning mother would sleep late and get up after the house would warm up.

Through the years of growing up mother had raised us girls to be ladies and we did not go out and do the farm labor, the boys did that. Gordon helped dad a lot around the farm. He worked hard milking the cows. The girls mostly stayed indoors and did the housework, read books and took walks. I liked to sew. Rosie loved music and spent a lot of time teaching little Judy to sing.

◆   ◆   ◆

We attended the Light House Mission church in Connersville. It was located on Court Street across from the Courthouse. That is where my family met the

Moore's. As it would turn out I would meet a nice good looking young man who was the oldest son of Daniel Boone and Emily (Rowland) Moore. The Moore family had come up from Owsley County, Kentucky for work. Helen (Moore) Jarnagin who was about the same age as me was a friend of mine in the Sunday school class. One Sunday after church she invited me over to visit her home. She told me, "Wait until you see my handsome brother who has beautiful eyes."

I did meet Herman Moore that day. Later he asked me if it would be possible for him and his father to come over to the farm on Thanksgiving Day and go hunting. As I recall the day my father did go hunting with Herman's father Daniel, but Herman didn't go hunting. I guess he was looking at another type of deer.

Herman became a wonderful part of our family. Many times he would drive his car down to the farm to visit me. He loved to bring candy for Judy as she was just a little girl. He would take us for drives and we would have a good time. Herman was still in high school when we met. Later he would graduate in the Connersville High School Class of 1940 and would be the first generation high school graduate in his family.

On Sundays after we returned from church everyone would help with the chores cleaning the dishes. Mother most always did the cooking and cleaning. Laundry was a separate day's work since we had to carry the water from the well and everyone had to help. We had a wash machine with handles that you had to pull back and forth. Albert and Gordon helped a lot with that part of the wash day. Mother hung out all the clothes outside. In the winter daddy wore long underwear and mother would hang them out to dry. They would freeze and when she would bring them in you could see them standing in the house.

In Albert's senior year the school offered a senior class trip. They went to Washington, D.C. on a bus. The route drove through the Shenandoah Valley, The Natural Bridge of Virginia, and on up to Niagara falls and was about a ten day trip.

The group went to the 1939 World's Fair in New York. He came home and was so excited to tell us all about what he had seen. Mother dearly loved Albert and they had a wonderful relationship. He worked one year as a machinist in Connersville at a local factory. He made about $23 a week. Other times he worked as a farm hand. Albert gave mother $5 a week for his room and board. Later he bought a brand new Model A Ford. He drove us kids around to places we had never been before. We went to Indianapolis and Chicago. World War II had begun and we would soon realize how much our lives would be changed by this war.

Rosie's senior class of 1940 took their trip to see the World's Fair in New York City, too. The school bus took eleven students and three adults on the trip. Rosie was a little fearful when she left but on the way she prayed that the Lord would deliver her from her fears so she could enjoy the trip. She asked the Lord directly to prove it to her by turning the rain into a sunny day. The next day the sun was brightly shining and her fear was gone away and from that point on Rosie was really happy throughout the entire trip. The group visited Washington, D.C. and war sites throughout Pennsylvania. Rosie is a natural journalist and made notes throughout the trip. Upon the groups return home, Rosie was the main speaker at the welcome back dinner where all the parents attended.

Mother dressed us well as possible. We didn't have new things but we had the best of the rummage sales. We had lots of fun growing up living on the farms. My mother may have had a hard life but she certainly didn't have to worry about her children. Her children were always an asset and she was very proud of us. Mother had a dream for each one of us. She wanted Albert to be a minister. She wanted Rosie to be a school teacher. She wanted Gordon to be a doctor. She wanted me to be a nurse. Mother didn't know exactly what Judy would be interested in achieving since Judy was still a young girl. Nevertheless Mother loved each one of her children.

Judy started first grade at Dunlapsville School while we still lived on the Egypt Hollow farm. She recalls one afternoon after getting off of the bus in front of the long snow covered lane. It was a very cold winter day. The lane was completely shut off with huge high snow drifts and heavy snow. Usually I would get off the bus with Judy, but this particular day I wasn't on the bus. Judy a small size little girl first noticed the snow drifts piled high up against the fence. She knew she couldn't make her way down the lane and didn't see any place to go except for the snow covered field. The bitter cold was more than she could bear. The only protection she had was her coat and little black shoes and brown stockings that only went up to her knees. Judy began to cry and feel very afraid when all of the sudden a big arm reached out and grabbed her. She was wrapped inside of a big green coat up next to a warm chest. She was covered with snow and couldn't make out who had come to help her. The big person carried her home and just a soon as she got inside she knew it was her daddy.

Judy enjoyed living on the farm in the country. She always would ask if she could take her shoes off and run in the fields. Finally one spring morning daddy told her she could go without her shoes. She ran through the yard and even in the fields.

We didn't have swing sets like children have today but that didn't stop Judy's imagination. One day she wondered what it would be like to slide down one of the tall stacks of freshly cut wheat. Everyday she would ask to get upon the giant haystack. Everyday the answer would be no, it's not settled yet. Then one day daddy said, "You can get up there now, it's settled." She made her way up the giant haystack and instead of sliding like she had imagined her body fell straight down and knocked the wind completely from her breath. Judy laid there for several minutes before she realized it wasn't a very good idea. You just can't slide down a haystack.

9

On Wings of Our Own

✦

1940–1942

After Rosie's graduation from high school in 1940 mother enrolled her in God's Bible School in Cincinnati. The school had an accredited Bachelor of Arts programs as well as religious training. Mother used the money Albert had paid to help Rosie acquire more education. Rosie stayed in the dorms and sometimes I got to go and visit the school as well. There were many wonderful people who attended there. The second summer Rosie had to stay at the school and work. The school required that every other summer students would stay on and help out with projects. I went down with Rosie during the summer and helped in the kitchen. Rosie worked in the office and I helped, too. We did projects like sending out mailers for the school.

Mother and Judy came down for a camp meeting during the summer. The meeting included services for children and mother attended the women's meetings.

Outside on the campus there were tables set up for showing and demonstrating all the mission work that was being done around the world. There was an American Indian who gave sign language while we sang "God Be with You until We Meet Again." It was the final service of the meeting and was just beautiful. Judy, who was a pre-schooler, remembers it to this day.

Rosie had many musical talents and it was at God's Bible School where she was introduced to the accordion. She told us how a young black girl who was a friend of hers had an accordion that she played. Rosie just thought it was a wonderful instrument. She asked the young girl if it would be okay to take the accordion back home to play for her parents on a weekend and yes, it was alright with her. Rosie stood in front of the mirror and learned to play the accordion on her own.

Rosie came home one weekend with the accordion and played it for mom and dad. They were so impressed that they bought her one and it cost around $125 which was a good sum of money then. Dad must have sold a pig to buy it for her. That was the only way dad could have raised a lump sum of money. Rosie has continued playing the Mother of Pearl accordion keys for over fifty years at churches, schools, and for many children.

Mother and dad never seem to mind all the times that Rosie and Albert had brought home boys and girls in big groups. They were mostly from God's Bible School.

Rosie ended up attending God's Bible School for two years. I remember one time we had eleven girls from Cincinnati staying with us for an overnight trip. They came up with Rosie on the Greyhound bus which we took on occasions. I can't remember exactly all the details, but I'm sure you wouldn't want to know. We didn't have indoor plumbing and all we had was an out house toilet.

Saturday evenings during the summer our fun times would be when the neighbor children and friends would all gather for an evening of music. Those who could play music brought their instruments and the rest of us would sing. Albert learned to play the guitar about the same time Rosie learned the accordion. He played the clarinet in school, too. We enjoyed the warm summer evening outside along the hillside singing and having a great time.

One summer dad bought Gordon a car. It was a 1934 black two door Chevrolet. Gordon had worked hard on the farm helping dad with the chores and he wanted to buy the car for him. Gordon had many friends one of which was Herb Kelley. It was in the early summer when Herb and Gordon decided they wanted to to California. So they set out driving Herb's 1932 four door Chevrolet. They drove to St. Louis where they hit an area of fog. Unable to drive they pulled over and spent the night in their car. The next day they went on and while driving through the State of Kansas they noticed a jack rabbit that had been killed in the road. Gordon being the farmer and hunter that he was wanted to stop and look at it. It was night so they put the rabbit in the trunk where the next day they would be able to give it a closer inspection. Arriving in Kit Carson, Colorado the boys discovered that the rabbit was infested with fleas and so was their entire car. They stopped by a gas station and asked how they could get rid of them and the man said with gasoline. So they doused the seats, the floors and just about the whole inside of the car. They couldn't stand to be in the car with the gasoline smell so they got a motel for the night and the next day they turned around and went back home.

Farming was slow and jobs were hard to come by. Gordon decided to join the CCC (Civil Conservation Corps) later that summer. This was a job paid by the government for men to go around and make improvements to the land. Managing soil erosion, planning of irrigation systems, and other programs that protected the land were some of the projects the CCC did. Another work group was called the WPA (Work Progress Administration) which made improvements in the towns and cities. In Connersville the WPA built the big reservoir system on top of Summit Avenue hill which stores water for Connersville. The WPA built the administration building, 4-H building and swimming pool in Roberts Park during this time period. Today the same pool still exists but is currently under consideration for replacing. Over time building do have to be replaced. These work programs were instituted to help supplement the unemployment due to the depression and help to build up our country.

Immediately after Gordon joined the CCC he was sent to Corydon, Indiana about 200 miles away from our home. He worked in the Harrison County State Forest. The group did forestry projects such as clearing the Chestnut trees and cleaning up the land. Gordon said some of the boys in his group seemed like they didn't know much, but they were hard workers. He stayed there about two months and decided the CCC just wasn't for him. Spring and summertime was hard on dad working the farm. He was experiencing poor health with what he thought was chronic sinus problems.

In the fall of Gordon's sophomore year in high school in Alquina he quit school to help dad gather and harvest the corn. Gordon earned his diploma from Alquina School by completing required courses while in the service. He worked at the Kroger's grocery store and before entering the service he was employed at a local factory working as a skilled riveter.

Grandpa Hiram, Grandma Sarah and Grace loved their new two story home which Grace had found to buy after Hiram had sold the two farms in 1937. The property was located in Lotus, about two miles east of Liberty, Indiana in Union County and had enough land for a garden and the cow they brought with them from the farm. The house was close to a railroad track. Grandma Sarah was a wonderful cook and she made delicious bread. She was a very loving grandmother who would always meet you at the door with hugs and kisses.

One Sunday morning in the summer of 1940, Grandpa Hiram and Grandma Sarah were all ready to leave their house to attend a family reunion that was held at the Roberts Park in Connersville. Grandma had packed a wonderful picnic basket full of fine foods such as fried chicken. Just as the family was leaving a man (bum as they were called in those days) walking hopelessly on the railroad track came up and asked if they had any food as he was hungry. Hiram said to him, "You stay here on the porch and I will be back." As I watched grandma open her basket of food, she made a plate of wonderful food just for the man. The bum would enjoy a portion of the same wonderful food that we would be enjoying that day at the family reunion.

10

The Years during W.W. II

◆

Spring 1942–1944

Mr. Graham had decided to sell the Egypt Hollow farm in the spring of 1942.

Albert went to join the service in September. Mother and dad had decided to move to town. They had arranged to borrow $500 from Albert to buy a home in Connersville. I was never aware that they had any plans to move to town. It was like a big secret. It was sometime in November that we began to look for a house to buy. It was then that they let us in on the secret. We all got to go to town and look around at the different houses. We kids were the ones that were instrumental in buying the big two story house on Summit Avenue in Connersville. The house was high upon a hill with some land so daddy could have a garden. If we wanted chickens there was even a place for them.

Daddy sold all of his farm equipment to the new owners of the Egypt Hollow farm. We moved between Christmas and New Years in 1942 to our new home on 135 Summit Avenue. My father got a job working in the casket factory. Later he went to American Central which was the aircraft factory and employed about 3,000 workers. He worked in the press room binding up the scrap metal. He worked twelve hours a day alternating every other week working days and nights all through the war years.

Albert had left his Model A Ford for mom and dad. He had bought it several years before from a girlfriend who was from Dublin. Her mother was widowed and had this brand new 1929 Model A Ford with only 500 miles on it. It was a wonderful car and we kept it for 5 or 6 years.

Mom was really excited when we moved to town. It was a pleasure to live in town after living on the farms most of her married life. Early in January the May-flower Van from what used to be the Poe Furniture store, not any relation to us, moved all of our belongings, furniture and the garden equipment that daddy had kept to our new house. The house we were moving into really wasn't a new house. It was an older house that had been built in 1875 and was a fine house. We liked the house.

The 2-story house had 3 bedrooms upstairs, one bathroom, and a basement, a small kitchen with an enclosed back porch off from it, dining room, a sitting room, and a parlor. There were French doors that opened into the parlor. The house was too big to heat all the rooms and many times the parlor was shut off. Daddy bought a big gas space heater that helped to heat the house. The heater pipe provided heat upstairs for the main bedroom but hardly sufficient for total comfort of the other two bedrooms.

I remember going to bed in the west bedroom the first night we stayed in the house and I had no idea it would be as cold as it was. I had been used to small rooms that were usually warm. It was the coldest night I ever spent in my whole life. The house was just clap board with no insulation. Wintertime in Indiana can be really cold!

I registered for high school which was located on Grand Avenue in town. Judy was entering her second grade of school. Daddy walked her down the hill to attend Fifth Street Elementary School. He showed her the way she would walk and from then on she walked to school.

The property was spacious for being in town. We had an extra lot that went up towards the top of the Summit Hill. We had space for a nice garden. The chicken house was towards the south of the house past the garden space. There was a garage along the side of the alley back to the north side of the house. The house sat next to an alley. In the back we had a nice yard. On the west border in the backyard was a hot bed used for starting seedlings. Dad raised some of his seedlings for the coming spring gardens. It had a glass cover so the sunshine could come through and produce healthy plants.

To the southwest of the house George and Bertha planted Cumberland Raspberries because they were a good source for a cash crop. Mother had customers for the raspberries. She would pick the berries and deliver them. She worked very hard to pick the raspberries and often times her face was a red as the raspberries. She really suffered from the heat. The money they made on cash crops supplemented their income.

Dad many times walked to work. Gas rationing was imposed for conserving gas because our county was at war now. You were given extra gas if you had to drive to work and had another passenger riding with you. Even though there was gas rationing due to WW I, Dad would once a month, usually on a Sunday afternoon, take the car and head to Liberty, Indiana to visit his parents. He was very close to his parents having worked with his father in the farming years.

Gordon and Rosie had started working at the aircraft factory by this time. American Central had started production and jobs were plentiful in town. Since Rosie return from God's Bible School she wanted to make money. She had just been through some lean years of college expenses and money was tight. Workers at the aircraft factory worked six days a week. They worked ten hours a day for five days and eight hours on Saturday and sometimes Sunday.

The summer of 1942 was my last carefree summer of driving around with Herman in his '36 Ford. We went so many places around the area and had such good times together. I knew he loved me very much and we talked of getting married after the war was over. By the end of the summer Herman joined the army and was gone to basic training. His army camp was located in North Carolina and we were getting homesick to see each other. He was afraid he would be shipped overseas without getting a furlough. He wrote his mother and asked her to bring me and come down for a weekend visit. I kept telling my mother I was going to go but she really didn't believe me. When I went she thought this would really be the end of me. But it really wasn't. Herman's mother, Emily and I went on the train. We rode all night to Atlanta and then got on the Seaboard Railroad to finish the trip back up the coast to Charlotte, North Carolina. We got there after dark on a Friday evening. Herman was not there to meet our train.

Mrs. Moore had misgivings about this time but I looked out the darkened window of the station across the open lot I could see the form of a person with a certain swing of his arm, as the cigarette in his hand brightened by the air currents. I knew it was Herman coming. We stayed in a private southern home and had such a good time for just two days. He trained for 18 months in the states and then to the European War area where he served in 5 major battles. His military occupational assignment was Radio Operator. We wrote many letters to each other during his time away. I still have some of the letters. I was sixteen years old when Herman left for World War II.

◆   ◆   ◆

Albert was drafted on September 11, 1942. He entered the Coast Artillery where he would learn Morris Code/Radio. In basic training Albert contacted an eye virus that caused him problems. He had been training in swampy areas to help prepare him for overseas duty. As a result of the eye infection he spent almost the better part of a year at Walter Reid Hospital in Washington, D.C.

Albert met Almeda (Anderson) at a church gathering in Richmond, Indiana and they had their first date in the summer of 1941. They were married in Connersville, Indiana on July 10, 1943 at the Nazarene Church.

Albert & Almeda (Anderson) Britton Wedding Day 1943
Left to right back row: Portia Wilson, Erma Britton, Harold Grimes, Rosie Britton, & Letha Mains
Front row: Judy Britton, Albert & Almeda Britton

Albert was on leave when they married and soon after the wedding he and Almeda returned to Washington, D.C. They found Almeda an apartment on the edge of the city in Maryland. She would ride the bus to visit Albert who was still recovering at Walter Reid Hospital and soon he was released. On September 11, 1943 Albert was discharged from the service.

In February 1944, Albert enrolled in a veterans program for education. Albert and Almeda moved to Fort Wayne, Indiana. He attended Indiana Technical University where he graduated summa cum laude (w/highest praise) with a Bachelor of Engineering majoring in Radio/Television. He was named to Phi Beta Kappa Honor Fraternity.

Albert worked for General Electric and Hughes Aircraft over his employment years as an Engineer and their family lived in Ohio, Pennsylvania, California and Arizona. Some of his assignments included development projects, working in the US space program and teaching positions.

Gordon enlisted for World War II duties in the spring of 1943. He was nineteen years old when he left. Two of his buddies, Russ and Herb, also volunteered for service. Gordon had hoped to get into the U.S. Air Force since he had been building airplanes at the factory. After arriving at Fort Harrison he was assigned to the Medical Corps (medics). He left for Santa Fe, New Mexico in the middle of May 1943 where he began his training at Bruns General Hospital for six months. The unit moved to Southern California for desert training and Gordon served as a Medical Technician. He helped to set up a hospital and worked in ambulance duties caring for the infantry who couldn't handle training in Death Valley.

After Gordon's service in the desert he was selected for Dental Technician School which also trained him in the area of x-ray. In the class of about three hundred Gordon graduated in the top twenty. His unit arrived in England on D-Day June 6, 1944 when the Allied forces landed in Normandy, France. He worked in one of the ten big hospitals that handled war casualties. One night his hospital received over thirteen hundred wounded soldiers. They all worked throughout the entire night carrying stretchers and by morning Gordon had blisters over his entire hands. His unit was awarded the Meritorious Service from General Dwight Eisenhower. Gordon's military service continued in the Reserves and during the Korean War from September 1950–September 1951.

Everyone did their part during the years our country was at war. Mother even worked at the aircraft factory. She wanted to earn enough money to buy new furniture for our house on Summit Ave. I watched Judy for Mother that summer.

In the year 1943 not many men stayed around our town. Most of them were gone to war. We met visitors from Kentucky who were attending our church. They were John and Lulu McKinney from Falmouth, Kentucky. John had three sons Elmo, Shelby, Johnny and three daughters, too. They were visiting John's sister Lucille and her husband Loren McMichael who attended our church.

We liked this family because they were from Pendleton County where Grandpa Hiram had lived. Elmo was the oldest boy in this family. My sister, Rosie had met Elmo but soon he left for the war. Shelby was sixteen and not old enough for war duties. Rosie and Shelby became friends. She was a few years older than Shelby but they didn't seem to mind that.

There weren't many things to do around town during the years of the war. There was, however, a stable on top of Eighth Street hill that had horses. Mr. Herbert owned riding horses at the stable. Rosie and I would go riding on horses that we rented from Mr. Herbert. We considered that our main recreation. Often we would ride two or three time on a weekend. We would ride just around the town, up at the park, and in the country. We even rode in a couple of horse shows. It was in the fall that a friend of mine James Miller was home from the service. He liked me but I was already in love with Herman and he knew he had no chance with me. We decided we wanted to ride the horses to Lotus just east of Liberty, Indiana to see my Grandma Sarah and Grandpa Hiram Britton. It was about 15 miles. Dad said to us, "If you do that I'm not taking any responsibility for what you are doing." He wouldn't tell us not to go but he didn't like the idea. Well Rosie, James and I went anyway against my father's better judgment.

Mr. Herbert said, "You will have to take the big horses not the pintos, like the ones you have been riding." The three of us went over to Liberty on the horses. It was a day Rosie didn't have to work. I guess I wasn't scheduled for school that day. We went on the main road to Liberty. Our horses had shoes and we rode along the side of the road. We got there about noon. They didn't know we were coming and grandpa was thrilled to death to have some horses to feed. Grandma fixed us a nice lunch. We didn't stay very long and we turned around and went back. Rosie was always the instigator and did everything she wanted to do. I was always the shy one and afraid to do anything. We were approaching the last hill going into Connersville when Rosie and this young fellow had the horses in the middle of the road which was State Rd 44 and began to run the horses down the hill as fast as they could go. I saw those two horses throwing their hind legs up going down the hill and I thought those two people where crazier than a hoot owl. I wouldn't have no more run my horse down the hill for fear he would fall down. They made it down the hill and we were home by 5:00 p.m.

The ride over to Liberty that day took the skin right off the inside of my legs. That night I went to the movies with James Miller. We went to The Auditorium Movie Theater and sat in the balcony on seats covered with mohair. I'm telling you that mohair just dug into my flesh like I'll never forget.

We didn't go very much in those days. Rosie was able to keep some of the coupons for the extra gas she was given because she had riders in her car. The Ford car didn't use a lot of gas. We took a few trips. One winter day we went down to Cincinnati to God's Bible School for the weekend. Another time we drove the car over to Greensburg where there was a lake. This was in the summertime. We stayed in a local hotel and enjoyed a two day vacation. One year we took the train to Detroit, Michigan to see my cousin Charlotte (Smith) Evans. We spent a few days up there. This was the extent of our vacations.

Before I graduated from High School in 1944, I worked at American Central which was the aircraft factory. I worked in the office and daddy worked out in the plant. He worked in the scrap area where they made the jeeps. On the other side of the plant they were making the wings for the Vultee Vengeance Dive Bombers aircraft. Rosie worked in this area that was called sheet metal.

Mother had taken Red Cross Volunteer training and was in the first class of Nurses' Aides. She volunteered at the local hospital and gave bedside care morning and afternoon to the patients. She was tender-hearted and sympathetic to sick people, especially the children. The hospital offered her a paid job several years later to work in the nursery, but she declined the opportunity so she could stay with Judy and my dad.

Judy had many musical talents, too. She learned to play the violin and liked to go and hear Marshall Kirk play his fiddle. When dad heard that Judy had an interest in learning to play the violin he encouraged her to take lessons in school. Judy said that George didn't realize that Marshall's playing was much like bluegrass. Daddy wanted her to play the violin in a classical manner. Even though Judy did learn to play the violin she enjoyed singing more. Everyone loved her beautiful voice.

Mother and dad didn't visit our schools often, but Judy remembers the day Bertha walked into her classroom. She was wearing a seal skinned fur coat with a gold sequined black hat looking very attractive. Judy's classmates whispered to her, "Your mother is very pretty." Mother never attended any of the PTA meetings when Judy was in school. Judy said later that she would have loved it if her mother could have been more involved in her school activities.

◆   ◆   ◆

Grandpa Hiram and Grandma Sarah Britton lived to see their 66th wedding anniversary. They were still living in the farm house just east of Liberty, Indiana at Lotus. It was the fall of 1944 that Sarah's heart began to fail her. Everyone seemed to know that the end of Sarah's life might be coming shortly. She had many visitors within a week as she was drifting into and out of consciousness. One time she came out of unconsciousness and said, "Oh, I've been to heaven. I got there and I saw all the people. They motioned for me and said I have to go back that I didn't get to stay." She said, "I saw everybody over there in heaven except for Frank".

A believer such as my Grandmother Sarah and many others we know of today pray for those who haven't made a public confession of their belief and faith in Jesus Christ. In our minds and hearts we pray that all will gather one day for a heavenly reunion in God's Kingdom where there will be no end!

It was at the end of the week that Sarah who was conscious at the time told her son, George Britton, not to pray for her to stay here because she wanted to go on to heaven. It was during the weekend that Hiram told Grace to go and make grape juice and bread for he wanted Grace to administer the elements of communion to them. And Grace did. Sarah was ready for heaven and wanted to go. She told Hiram not to keep her here because she was ready. It was as though he had to release her before she could die. Hiram said to her, "I will not eat of the fruit of the vine or eat the bread until I drink it with my Father who is in heaven." These are the words Jesus said at the Last Supper when He was with his disciples.

Sarah Elizabeth (Poe) Britton died Monday afternoon September 11, 1944 at her home in Lotus. She was 84 years old. Her funeral was held in The Church of the Nazarene in Connersville, Indiana and she is buried in the Dale cemetery.

Sarah Elizabeth Poe and Hiram Pierce Britton were blessed with 24 grandchildren and 21 great grandchildren at the time of Sarah's death. An original poem written by Grace Britton is printed in the back of this book titled:

"The Day after Christmas at Grandma's"

◆   ◆   ◆

My mother was a wonderful cook and many times offered to prepare meals for church speakers and visiting guests. We had a representative at The Nazarene Church who was from Olivet Nazarene College, Kankakee, Illinois. Mother was asked to serve a meal at the Britton home for the guests that were recruiting students for the college. Little did we know the speaker coming for the weekend was the President of Olivet College. Mother served a delicious meal for the Sunday after church gathering.

I had graduated from Connersville High School in the spring of 1944 and began working at the aircraft factory in the office. Rosie was ready for a change; she too was working at American Central. The Olivet Nazarene College President, Dr. A. L. Parrett encouraged us to consider attending the school there in

Illinois. We were at a decision making time in our lives. I consider now that our decision we made that weekend was a prime mistake.

Rosie said she wanted to do something else and didn't want to go. She didn't want to sacrifice and not have anything like it was during the last two years of being in college. By now for the first time in Rosie's life she had all brand new clothes, coats, suits, shoes, rainwear, everything. She had earned money while working at the aircraft factory and had saved money, too. She decided to quit the aircraft factory and join The Waves. Rosie joined The Waves in September 1944. The Waves was a branch of the Navy for women in the military. Her boot camp training was at Hunter College in New York City. She was very happy to be part of The Waves. Christmas was very nice for her that year when she even got her own stocking filled with candy and an orange. Growing up underprivileged just made you appreciate even the smallest things in life.

After Rosie's boot camp training her group traveled on a secret mission by night train up into Canada and back down into Iowa. She enrolled at Iowa State Teachers College where she attended school for a semester. Times were fun for her at Iowa College. She rode in a one horse open sleigh over a beautiful winter snow and enjoyed new and exciting winter sports. Eventually Rosie was assigned to the Navy Department in Washington, D.C. working at the Bureau of Ordinance.

2nd Class Petty Officer Yeoman, Rosie Britton 1945

I would have gone to Olivet College if Rosie had decided to go there. I believe there would have been a way for us to go. We would have come up with the money somehow. Herman didn't like the idea of me going to college and told me in a letter that if I went he wouldn't be there for me. I did love him and he did show me a good time. Up to that time in my life my happiest moments were the things he did for me, gifts and places he took me before he entered the war. He had been gone now for about two years.

I worked at the aircraft factory for about a year until April 1945 when I joined the Civil Service and went to Washington, D.C. I remember arriving in Washington by way of train. It was a bright sunny day and the broad avenues stretched out at many angles from the Union Station. Only street cars and taxis were to be seen. There were few cars due to the gas rationing. It all looked so pretty and clean. I could see the Capitol Building and the fountain glistening in the sunshine. Immediately, I loved it all.

Rosie was there in Washington working in the Bureau of Ordinance which procured all the fire power for the Navy. The Civil Service, which I worked in, took care of their people and helped them to find places to stay and situated in their jobs. I found a place to live. You didn't have to be special to join the Civil Service as there were many people in demand. There were thousands of women working in Washington, D.C. for the war effort. I asked to be in the Bureau of Ordinance as Rosie was working for the Navy there. They did place me there.

The Navy workplace building was white and a block long and six stories high. That was all the Bureau of Ordinance. The building was located close to Constitution Avenue and bordered along The Reflecting Pool. The war seemed to be winding down in Europe and the Allied Forces were winning. Our dear President Roosevelt who led us to recovery from the great depression and to near victory of the Great War had just died the month before and a new President, Harry Truman had taken his place in the White House. The White House seemed very drab to me and in fact they had painted it gray for security purposes and hung black out curtains at the windows. It was closed to the public for the duration of the war and none of the lovely national shrines were lit and certainly not the Capitol Building. Even in war times Washington was still a beautiful place with its parks and fountains. I especially felt greatly honored to be there in an historical time.

Rosie and I worked through the day and ate lunch together. We walked and enjoyed ourselves as carefree young people. I stayed in the area six months.

One hot sticky evening I arrived home at my apartment with a message waiting for me. Mother and Judy were arriving in the city the next morning on the train to spend a week with us. On such a quick notice I wondered where I would put them. My landlord allowed them to stay with me on the adjoining sun porch and together we all toured the city and had a really fine time.

Daddy never came out to see us in Washington. By now he too was employed at the aircraft factory and would never leave his job. He worked very hard there with long hours. Bertha's mother, Emma said once to him, "George don't you know you're shortening your life by working a two man's job when you work twelve hours a day." Dad just said to her, "Well it's all right because these boys are over seas and they're giving their lives so I do what I can do." As it turned out George put all the extra money he made during those years working 12 hours a day towards his house on Summit Avenue. The bankers commented that they wouldn't make very much interest on George Britton because he put as much as possible on his loan. He didn't know it at the time but as events would unfold it was God's blessing for him to have the house on Summit Avenue paid for.

11

Victory & New Beginnings

❖

1945–1946

Rosie and I were in Washington when VE day (Victory over Europe) came on May 7, 1945. I hadn't been in Washington more than a month. It didn't seem to matter to us much because we were still facing the big Pacific War. The atmosphere in the streets was as usual except for a few pockets of jubilation. Washington was full of returning war heroes and we often were allowed to leave our job for a turn out in the street to welcome home some dignitaries.

We saw General "Skinny" Wainwight come home to a heroes welcome. Bunting adorned the light poles and bands played while this dear man rode in an open car to wave to the crowds. Never in my life had I seen so frail a person. He had been a prisoner of the Japanese and was on the Death March from Bataan to Corregidor and nearly starved as did many of our troops in the early days of the Pacific War.

Then we saw General Bradley and Admiral Nimitz and finally General Eisenhower came. The streets filled with cheering crowds and the sky would fill with planes to add to their welcome. The platform built for the welcoming ceremony for General Eisenhower was just down from our work building. We stood very near the railing to see John and Mayme along with the General when he delivered his speech. These were great days to be in Washington and here I was just a little farm girl from Bear Creek getting to witness all this. How my heart swelled within me.

The real end of World War II came on September 2, 1945 when the Japanese formally surrendered to the Allies on aboard the U.S. battleship Missouri. America had dropped two atomic bombs on Japan at Hiroshima and Nagasaki in August 1945.

The day the first bomb hit there was a hush on the streets as people read most earnestly the account in the paper of the great bomb which had been dropped over the city of Hiroshima in Japan. It was the most awesome thing anyone had ever heard of. It laid waste a whole city and killed thousands and had burned the entire city. The paper read of things like splitting the atom and radioactivity and fearsome things none of us had ever heard of. This was the beginning of the nuclear age. This bomb had been developed in Nevada and New Mexico. It had been an absolute secret development of the military. President Truman had given his command to use this weapon to bring about the end of the war in Japan.

Already our war weary troops from the European area were on their way to the Pacific Theater of Operations. Our President knew that without an end to the war many of these troops would never live to come home. He saw a long bloody struggle ahead and gave his permission to use the bomb to end the war.

I'll never forget that day in the office. We hardly worked at all. We all sat and read our papers, talked and waited for an end to the war. It did not come. We could not believe that this Japanese nation would continue under this terrible attack. We waited one day, two days, and three days and finally we heard. Another bomb had been dropped on another Japanese city. How horrifying. This time the Japanese nation laid down its arms. They surrendered.

The news came that the war was over, I hurried from my apartment and down the avenue a few blocks to the front of the White House. The streets were so full of cheering crowds, one could hardly walk. We stood across the street in Lafayette Square and sang, danced, and yelled. We asked for "Harry" but the President did not come to the window. I never did see the President while I was in Washington, but he gave the work weary government workers a three day holiday. How we did enjoy this time! Hugging and kissing and joy in the streets. All the eating places were closed in the government office buildings and for more than a day we would not get anything to eat. It was bedlam. After a day or so, I was able to get across the city to the area where Rosie lived in the Navy Barracks. Things finally settled down.

Troops had been arriving in New York for weeks now from Europe. Each day I would scan the papers to see if my honey, Herman's ship would arrive. How I wanted to be there when he got off the ship. We did see Gordon's unit had come into New York and he came to Washington to visit us. We saw a tired listless person, unimpressed by the great city of Washington. The small boy we knew before was no more. All he wanted to do was get home to the quietness of Indiana. We knew the war would change us all.

For weeks I had been getting letters from Herman. He was in southern France awaiting a ship to bring his outfit home. He visited Paris and waited some more. He wrote loving letters of how he wanted to get home and see me again. He wrote how he wanted us to be married. He even wrote to my dad, "Dear Pop" he said. I thought of all this and cried. Did I have the courage to be married and settle down to one person for the rest of my life?

I wanted to stay in Washington and meet Herman, but I was called home by my mother. My tour of duty was for six months and so I could return home now. Rosie and I wanted to go to New York City for a weekend adventure. We really didn't have the funds to stay overnight in a hotel. We decided to take a night train, visit New York in a day, and leave late that night. We arrived at the break of dawn and all the street sweepers were busy doing their jobs. We walked up the broad avenue from the Empire State Building to Rockefeller Center. In the Center we watched the skating and spent a lot of time at the top in its roof gardens.

We rode the subway to see The Statue of Liberty. There were ships docked as the troops were coming in. It was Navy Day and many people walked all the time in the streets and cars could not get through. Many great ships lay in the New York Harbor, row after row of great ships at anchor. It was as if the country had literally stopped in its tracks. We walked and walked and were so weary when we boarded the train to go back to Washington. Never had I seen such a city, it frightened me but we had to see it before returning to the mid-west.

I returned from Washington, D.C. early in November 1945. My mother's youngest brother, Arbie Ivan Clark, was dying of cancer. He was only thirty-seven years old. Mother had taken a bus to Fort Wayne, Indiana to visit Albert and Almeda who were expecting a baby. The birth of Sharon Rose Britton was on November 13, 1945. Bertha didn't get to stay and help out with the new baby very long. In fact she was only there a short time when I had to call mother to come home for the funeral of her youngest brother, Arbie, who had just died on November 16, 1945.

It would be several weeks before Bertha would get to see her new granddaughter again and George would hold Sharon for the first time. Albert said, "Mother was happy about Sharon's birth. She was always on my case for us to have a baby. We traveled a few times down to visit with my parents after the birth of Sharon," recalls Albert.

Herman came all the way home without even letting me know when he would be in Connersville. He called the same day that Uncle Arbie Clark died. I had waited for three years to see him. Herman was a handsome soldier home from the war, home at last. We said nothing just holding to one another with great love.

"Forever Yours, Herman" 1945

Herman and I married on December 15, 1945 at the Nazarene Church in Connersville. It was 5 degrees below zero and the roses were nipped by the cold. I was nineteen years old and he was twenty-four. The church was filled with over 200 people that cold evening. It was Christmas time and all my lovely attendants were dressed in gowns of white. They all carried red flowers and mine were white roses.

Herman and Erma (Britton) Moore Wedding Day 1945

We became parents of a beautiful baby boy who arrived on October 14, 1946 in Connersville, Indiana. My mother suggested his name be given David, which means beloved. We decided to name him David George after my father. He was the most perfect baby I have ever known in this world.

Herman and I were living in an apartment but soon bought a little house in Offutt's Park which was on the north side of Connersville. Herman worked at American Kitchens after the war and was assigned to the Engineering Department. He continued to work in electronics employed with Avco Corporation, Stant Manufacturing, and Indiana Ordnance. He still is a consultant on occasions for Indiana Ordnance.

I'd like to continue here a little about David. My mother dearly loved my son. He was very special to her. I went back to work at American Kitchens after David was born. Mother and Daddy wanted to care for him and they needed the extra money so I paid them to watch David. They watched him from age nine months until he entered the first grade.

David began first grade at the 5th Street School and after school he would walk to his other Grandmother Emily Moore's house on Fourth Street. This worked out better for him during the school year. During the summers David would stay at George and Bertha's house while I continued to work.

David remembers the story of how he fell through the glass greenhouse panels that George and Bertha used to grow their new garden seedlings on Summit Avenue. His legs were badly cut and mother sat him up near the kitchen sink with his legs hanging over dripping with blood down the drain. David cried, "Grandma I don't want to go to the hospital.' Bertha just couldn't stand the thoughts of her most loved grandchild going to the hospital and said to George she didn't think he would need stitches. He survived the accident with a scar on his leg. He can tell the story with proof to show.

◆   ◆   ◆

Rosie went back to Washington after my wedding since her military assignment hadn't finished yet. She had continued to correspond with Shelby McKinney who had joined the Navy at seventeen and was in Philadelphia by 1946. He was the younger man from Connersville whom Rosie had met and they had developed a friendship. Shelby's military assignment was on a ship that eventually took him around the world by age eighteen.

One day Rosie knew Shelby's ship the U.S.S. Tennessee, a battleship, was anchored in the harbor at Philadelphia. She was in Washington, D.C. at the time. Rosie took the train up to meet with Shelby. He was stationed on board the ship so she had to go aboard. She didn't know much about boarding a ship. Rosie stepped out of the taxi wearing her full dress military uniform which was high heel shoes, skirt, blouse, jacket and hat. Most people who pulled up in a taxi to board a ship were usually military officers.

Rosie wasn't an officer; she was an enlisted person with the rank of a 2nd class petty officer. She walked up the huge ship plank. Hundreds of U.S. Navy sailors that had just returned from over seas were just staring with intense curiosity. Who was this woman? They watched to see if she knew the protocol of boarding a U.S. Navy ship which was a salute to the officer of the deck. Rosie saluted and asked for permission to board the ship. Upon permission to board she turned and saluted the flag of the United States of America. All the sailors sighed and realized she meant business and knew exactly what to do. She asked to meet Shelby McKinney and they took her up and down ladders. She later said those officers and young sailors all must have got a big kick out of seeing me in my high heel shoes and skirt walking around the ship.

In the spring of 1946 Rosie and Shelby were married in Washington, D.C.

Rosie May (Britton) and Shelby F. McKinney—Wedding Day 1946

When they were discharged from the service they moved to Fort Wayne, Indiana. Albert and Almeda lived in Fort Wayne, too. Rosie's marriage to Shelby didn't last, she had been hurt and her hopes shattered. Albert encouraged her through this difficult time and Rosie prayed for God to lead her. She made the decision to return to college under the G.I. Bill for veteran's education. God did have a plan for her.

◆   ◆   ◆

While Gordon was stationed in England he met Vera (Hartill) a young beautiful woman who caught his attention immediately. Her family was of genuine qualities and just wonderful people and they made Gordon feel so welcomed. During the war many of the local people forbid their families especially their daughters to be attached to the American soldiers. This was the summer of 1945. Gordon fell in love with Vera and promised he would bring her and her family to the United States as soon as possible. She came the following summer to America by way of The Queen Mary, a grand ship! Gordon and Vera where married August 31, 1946 at the 4th Street Nazarene Church in Connersville, Indiana.

Gordon Britton & Vera (Hartill) Britton Wedding Day 1946

Gordon's career was working in x-ray and dental work. He operated Fayette County's first dental lab making teeth for all but one dentist in Connersville. Later he worked as a department head at Fayette Memorial Hospital in x-ray. Vera's family came to America in the spring of 1948. Frederick and Rosina Hartill along with their two other children, Ray and Brenda, were sponsored under immigration rules and they established their home in Connersville eventually becoming citizens of the United States. Fred died in 1971 and Rosina in 1982. Ray and Brenda still are living.

After Rosie's marriage ended she enrolled at Olivet College in Kankakee, Illinois in 1948. She studied for three years and graduated Magna Cum Laude (honors with great praise) with a Bachelor of Arts Degree in Elementary Education in 1951. Mother and I went to her graduation ceremony. We were so proud of her.

The summer following Rosie's graduation from college she and her girlfriend enrolled in a graduate level program in Colorado. They could enjoy a vacation along with pursing additional education. Later this would be another answer to Rosie's prayers.

I know I'm getting a little ahead of myself in the story. Please forgive me. The next few years of our lives would be changed dramatically with our children being born and George and Bertha becoming grandparents themselves. Life was hectic but ooh how the time goes so fast and can be the most wonderful years of life. This was the end of 1946; mother and dad living at the Summit Avenue house, Judy ending her grade school years, and all of us are now living on our own.

12

Bad News

✦

1947–1949

In 1947, with the war over, production at American Kitchens was slowing down. The name had been changed after the war to American Kitchens and workers were being laid off. It was about this time that daddy started to notice his vision was fading away. Things were darker in the factory and he couldn't see on his job as well. He was one of the many that was laid off during this time and he would never return after that.

Albert scheduled Dad an appointment with an optometrist in Fort Wayne. It seemed like nobody could tell George what was the matter with his eyes. By 1948 his vision was noticeably worst and he couldn't see well enough to drive his car. Ray Mains, a family friend, from our church commented, "George why don't you go over to Rushville? There's a doctor in that town that can tell you what is the matter with your eyes."

Daddy took his advice and went to see the doctor in Rushville and returned home that evening. We were sitting at the kitchen table and my mother was fixing big hamburgers. She made them something like meatloaf burgers. Daddy came in while we were preparing to eat our dinner. He stood beside the table and said, "I'm going blind. I've got glaucoma and I've had it for eight years. The doctor told me that sight lasts ten years if the glaucoma is not treated." This was the first time we learned the diagnosis of what was happening to our father's vision. We finished our dinner and daddy retired to his chair.

Glaucoma causes increased pressure within the eyeball and damages the optic nerve and there is gradually a loss of vision. The Rushville doctor sent him immediately to Indianapolis. Daddy started commuting back and forth to Indianapolis. He later felt that he was being treated as a guinea pig. They tried to operate on his worst eye by cutting a slit that would allow fluid to release, but it didn't work.

He ended up just using the eye drops, since the glaucoma had taken the toll on his eyes. These were really sad times. He was about 64 years of age.

Daddy wasn't able to find work, he wasn't old enough for social security and he didn't have a great deal of money. Mother was starting to withdraw within herself since the bad news of Daddy's vision. Judy was just entering her teenage years when our father was diagnosed with glaucoma and mother wasn't doing well handling the stress.

Throughout her high school years Judy watched her mother go down hill and eventually daddy lost his sight. This was hard on all of us children. This seems a good time to say that everyone should have their eyes tested and be aware of the seriousness of glaucoma.

Mother and Dad were struggling with finances. Money for the household budget was hard to earn. As a student in Junior High Judy didn't have many clothes. I made her some clothes she could wear to school. She only had one pair of shoes that lasted her through her junior high years. Mom packed Judy's lunch for school and it would be an egg sandwich most of the time.

Aunt Grace and Grandpa Hiram had continued to live in the two story house. It was on an October day in 1948 Hiram was cleaning off his garden area when he suddenly didn't feel well. Doctor Gordin was called to the house and told the family that Hiram would rest better at home than the hospital. Elsie and Grace stayed with him.

As Grace was leaving Hiram's room he said to her, "You tell 'em I'll meet them on the other side." He knew that Heaven was close at hand and as Grace walked on her way it suddenly hit her that her father was dying and he wanted her to tell everyone he would be there to meet them as they came into the Kingdom of Heaven someday.

Hiram died at the age of 88 on October 25, 1948. He was a true believer in Christ and a good man.

◆   ◆   ◆

Grace had cared for her parents all of her life never marrying. Both of them were gone and now she was alone in the house. She eventually sold the two story house in Lotus to move to Connersville. She never made mention to any of the family members on the sale of the household goods. There was a baby grand piano that had a Victrolla, a record player, in it. It was one of only two made in Laurel, Indiana. Hiram enjoyed old time music and fiddle tunes having been brought up in Kentucky. I'm sure he owned some early records of country music.

Grace was a good Christian woman who taught Sunday school at the Nazarene Church. She was supportive of her parents and very faithful to the end.
Grace died on July 26, 1961 and is buried in Dale Cemetery in the family plot
near her parents. She was sixty-six years old.

Grace Ellen Britton 1937

13

Life in the 1950's

◆

1950–1967

Bertha and George had lived on Summit Avenue for several years now. The house had modern conveniences such as indoor plumbing and a toilet in an upstairs bathroom. The refrigerator was a little different than we know of today. It was called an ice chest. The ice man would come and put a block of ice in it everyday or so. Eventually they did have a modern day refrigerator which was located off the kitchen in a back room. Mother shopped at the A & P grocery store in Connersville. She liked sweets and always bought donuts. At home she baked delicious gingerbread spice cake with 7-minute frosting. She loved soda pop and ice cream.

Mother enjoyed working puzzles and playing records on their 78 speed record player. It was about the 1950's that households began to have television sets, however my parents never owned a TV. Their main interests were studying the Bible and teaching Sunday school adult Bible classes. They attended the Nazarene Church and on some occasions went to Evangelical United Brethren church. For several years the minister of the Nazarene church who lived outside of Connersville at that time enjoyed Sunday after church dinner at my parents house. This seems like a good place to tell you mother's favorite song was *"Under His Wings"*.

Dad continued to plant his garden and harvest their food. Howard Clark, mother's brother, would come with his tractor to plow and disk the garden. Mother would help by laying out the first row with string tied to stakes. Then daddy would plant the row and move the stakes to make the next row. They often worked hard together raising the crops that they would sell to their customers. They continued to raise the Cumberland Raspberries which mother would sell.

Daddy read the newspaper until 1952 when he could only see one word at a time through his pipe stem vision. He got to the point that he couldn't see what line he was on when he was reading the newspaper. It was then when George quit reading the newspaper. He was sixty-eight years of age by now.

Dad listened to the radio to keep up with the news of the day. I remember when our family purchased our first radio which was about January 1943. It was a walnut table-top model about 17"x9"x9" that dad bought at the Goodyear store. We did have a phone which had been installed during the WWII years.

My dad was a profile of courage through the lost of his vision. He never complained or felt self pity. He told his minister if I lose my sense of humor I will have lost it all. Dad just continued to enjoy his life and was always a blessing to many. He loved to tell stories and most of them were Bible stories. He was a true testimony of the living presence of God in the human flesh.

After the loss of his vision things that dad could do before he couldn't do now. Tasks such as mowing the yard would be done by Gordon and his sons. They used push mowers back then. We knew finances for mom and dad was very difficult now that dad had lost his vision. None of us had very much money to help out with our parents. They always had a bank account but not much money. Dad received $52 per month on social security. We all pitched in to help pay the taxes on their home. Rosie got $75.00 per month for her room and board while she was pursuing her education through the G.I. Bill. Rosie sent money home to help. Judy got about $14 from social security because dad was blind. Mom and dad lived on very little money.

In 1951 Rosie accepted a teaching position in the small town of St. Anne, Illinois which was just outside Kankakee. She taught sixth grade her first two years there. Rosie was in her early thirties by now and felt there was no future in the small town. She began to pray and ask the Lord to guide her in the direction He wanted for her life. She said the Lord spoke to her and definitely told her she had to go back to Connersville. She said to the Lord, "But Lord I don't want to go back to Connersville!" Always the message would come back that she was to go back home to Connersville. In 1953 she returned driving her 1951 Starlight Studebaker and began teaching for the Fayette County School Corporation. She taught for two years until her life took another turn.

It wasn't long before she heard that Shelby who was back in Kentucky wanted to see her again. Shelby had a little daughter now, her name was Debbie. He had been married and divorced again. His mother was sick and he was eager to talk with Rosie. It was then that Shelby came back into Rosie's life. The church people and most everyone tried to tell Rosie that she shouldn't get involved with the man who had caused her so much grief in the past. Rosie desired children of her own and longed for a family. They were married in the spring of 1954.

Shelby dreamed of going west to California and Rosie liked the idea of moving away from Connersville. They drove her little car to California. Shelby attended Nazarene College in Pasadena and later a community college but sadly was returning to his old lifestyle. He worked at several different jobs and the family income was low most of the time.

They had four children who were born in California. After ten years things were beginning to fall apart and life for the family was increasing unbearable. The children were hungry, sickly and Rosie herself was at the very bottom physically and emotionally. My father told Rosie she had to come home. California was so far away from her family. She made the decision to return home again to Connersville.

Herman and Gordon drove our big station wagon over the Thanksgiving holiday in 1963 to California where they would pick up five children and Rosie. Debbie was also making the trip back to live with her Grandmother in Kentucky. All the children were under the age of 10. Attached to the car was a little trailer. They traveled miles and miles on snow and iced covered roads. It was an exhausting trip of hours of straight driving but everyone arrived back safely.

Rosie stayed at our home until February when we all helped to get her a little place of her own. It was like a miracle that all the household items she needed just came in at the same time from various friends and relatives and once again the little family was together in their own home. Rosie and Shelby were divorced in 1964. Rosie was hired again by the Fayette County School Corporation teaching elementary education. She worked and raised her children and provided a wonderful Christian home. Rosie taught 30 years in four states until her retirement.

◆   ◆   ◆

Judy began her high school years in 1950. She met Lowell Roettger at Miller Dairy an ice cream store in Connersville. Mom and Dad liked Lowell and accepted him very well. Most of her friends were from the Nazarene church and Lowell did attend with her on occasions. He helped Judy get a job at Miller Dairy and she worked there during her high school years. She made .35 per hour and supported herself throughout high school. Often times Judy felt alone and on her own, dad being blind and mother not very well. Judy recalls Dad raising the most wonderful delicious popcorn. Many evenings Judy and Lowell would enjoy popping corn and working on their lessons together. Lowell graduated in May 1953 and joined the U.S. Marine Corps where he served two years.

Judy was disappointed that mom and dad wouldn't get to attend some of the highlights of her high school years. She sang a solo in her baccalaureate service. Mom and Dad didn't attend her graduation; I don't know why, other than mother might have been sick. Judy graduated in the National Honor Society in the Connersville High School class of 1954.

She went to Cincinnati, Ohio for training to be a nurse. Every weekend she was off she would return home to help mother and daddy who had many needs. She was a blessing for them as she would practice singing in the parlor and help them with their needs. Judy soon realized that it was too much for her to handle the stress of learning and the worry of her parents. She decided to quit nurses training and return to Connersville.

It was December 31, 1954 when Lowell and Judy were married at Grand Avenue United Methodist Church. Our little sister was now married.

Sarah Judith (Britton) and Arthur Lowell Roettger Wedding Day 1954

Judy and Lowell resided in Connersville the rest of their married life. They had three children. Lowell was trained in plant maintenance and employed as a maintenance superintendent at the Ford Electronics and Refrigeration Corporation plant in Connersville. Judy raised her children, attended additional college classes, was manager of the local Red Cross, and tutored elementary school aged children. Judy and Lowell were married over forty-one years until cancer took the life of Lowell in 1996.

Lowell was a fine gentleman who worked hard and served his community through his leadership in programs such as the boy scouts. He was a devoted father and grandfather and gave his all to his family. Lowell supported the church and helped to organize a Sunday school class. He was much needed after his retirement but God in His plans for Lowell took him home. We have missed him these past years.

◆   ◆   ◆

Mother learned to drive after dad lost his vision. My son David recalls many good times with Grandma Bertha Britton. He remembers especially the 1948 Studebaker car that most of the time was parked in the garage just off the alley by the house. Everyday around the same time of the day Bertha would take him for a ride. It wasn't a long drive just a few miles to the west towards what was called "Bunker Hill". It was at this point that Bertha would turn the car around and drive back home to Summit Avenue. David believes that his grandmother being the only driver of the car since George had gone blind by now wanted to keep up her driving skills. It must have been a good feeling of security that she knew how to drive and was able to get around when the need would arise.

It may seem somewhat insignificant to tell all of you about Grandma Britton's tower but for many of us who remained living in Connersville, we recall these visions. On top of the hill just above George and Bertha's Summit Avenue home was a landmark tower which reached well into the sky and provided radio communications for the area. Travelers approaching from the west of Connersville on State Road 44 could see this tower for many miles before they arrived into the city. Vacations were a luxury most people didn't take or couldn't afford but when our travels took us away from our hometown we were generally gone for about one week. For small children a week away from home can seem like a very long time. Anxiously longing for home and excited to be returning to familiar surroundings the children would spot the tower several miles away coming back home from the west. "There's Grandma's tower" they would shout and happiness would fill our car as we returned home from vacations. In the 1950's there were very few communications towers, but today the horizons are often filled with towers rising to the sky.

Dad had a real love for being outside where he could enjoy the fresh air, meditate and listen to the sounds of God's world. He would go outside and sit in his spring-loaded steel rocking chair and feel the sunshine on his skin. The birds would sing and he would listen. You would be surprised how much you can hear when you close your eyes.

George loved to sing and was very good. His memory was fabulous and he loved the old songs. Songs like "*The Old Rugged Cross, Amazing Grace, What A Friend We Have in Jesus, The Ninety Nine, My Savior First Of All,* were some of his favorites. The neighbors across the street who heard him sing just loved to listen. The words in the songs went through his voice and his heart was blessed. Even though his vision was gone his sight was expressed though the strong mind that God had given him. His testimonies through music and words caused people to change their lives. A neighbor lady once told us the Holy Spirit spoke to her heart though the songs she would hear George Britton sing and she gave her heart to Jesus Christ. She died much earlier than my Daddy and went to heaven long before he ever did.

We are not sure how the lost of Daddy's vision effected Bertha's health. The lost of a person's vision is a devastating occurrence. She was emotionally upset but always kept her faith in Jesus Christ. She was a wonderful person who cared deeply for her family and her friends. She was a devoted and hard-working Christian wife, and mother who inspired her children to reach for high Christian goals.

About 1954, Mom began to experience hallucinations and imagined things that were not real. Indianapolis doctors said in 1956 they believed she had hardening of the arteries in her brain. They thought she had malnutrition. They put her on vitamin D and vitamin B shots. The doctors treated her with tranquilizers which were widely used in the mental hospitals at that time. The problem seemed to be in the front of her brain and not necessarily any disease that could be diagnosed. She was fifty-nine years old.

Mom and dad lived alone in the house on Summit Avenue now that Judy was married. In fact all of George and Bertha's children were now raising their own families. There were still some fun times to live through the years on Summit Avenue.

Grandchildren were born; eventually there would be a total of twenty-one grandchildren of George and Bertha Britton.

The children especially enjoyed the stories George would tell them. They were impressed with how their blind grandpa could do many things even without the use of his eyes. He was known to have the Bible almost memorized. You could ask him anything about the Bible and he would know the story and exactly where he could tell you to look in the Bible. He told other stories, too.

If you would ask the grandchildren about their grandpa, one thing that stands out in their minds is that they would remember the power he had through his prayers. You would never begin a meal and eat at the table without first bowing your head to pray and ask the Lord's Blessings on the food.

The upstairs of the house on Summit Avenue was an inviting place for the children. There were windows you could look out and see way down the hill and out in the back yard. The feather bed was always so nice and fun to play on. Some would remember the bathroom that didn't have a closet door but had shelves behind a curtain.

It was a spacious upstairs with a door opening to the attic. The downstairs parlor was arranged with beautiful furniture and flowery carpeting throughout. The parlor area was saved for special occasions, wedding parties, and music was enjoyed in this area. David practiced piano lessons there and Rosie played music, too.

It's the simple routines and lifestyles the grandchildren remember about their grandpa and grandma's home. George had a glass salt holder on the kitchen table and being blind he would reach for the salt with his fingers and feel for the amount he would need for his meal. Many times when you visited the Summit Avenue home you would find grandpa laying his head on the big gas stove in the front living room as he was resting in a chair enjoying the comfort of the warm air. In the same room with him was Bertha sitting in her rocking chair. She would use her foot to keep the chair continually rocking. Sometimes the grandchildren would be ill and grandpa and grandmas would be a place for them to get well until they could return to school. A big sofa provided a comfortable bed to lie until the ailment would leave them and they would return to health.

The house was always a welcome spot for the toddlers to exercise their active little legs by running like the lightning throughout the house. Laughter filled the dining room area on the Christmas that mother received a toilet seat for a present. Chocolate pudding and ice cold coke in the refrigerator treated youngsters home after a long day at school. Some days Bertha would go to the closet reach up and get into her black purse for pocket change. She would instruct the visiting grandchildren to go down to Hill Top Market and buy some ice-cream which was a real favorite of hers. The store was only a short distance down the hill from the house.

Mom and dad would require our help with certain chores. I would go grocery shopping, Judy would do the laundry, and Gordon would handle the medicine. We all helped out in different areas. We saw to the needs of our parents.

Judy remembers it was about 1965 when she found mother in a bad way. Mother wasn't able to take care of her personal needs like washing her hair and other things. It was then that we realized that mother would require a home caregiver. Mrs. Wilma Handley was a wonderful Christian woman who was recommended to our family to help my parents with housekeeping. Wilma became a strong backbone for help in our family. She was the extra hand we needed and was God's gift to us. She would fix breakfast for them and see to their needs. In the mornings she would cook food for their evening meals, something that my dad could warm up on the gas stove.

I don't know exactly everything she did, but Wilma was the brightest spot in our life at that time. Our families were not wealthy and most of us were raising our children and money was tight. We were able to collectively gather funds to pay Wilma for the care she gave to our parents. We paid her $100 per month. She stayed helping our family for several years.

Mother had a cataract removed from her eye in 1968. Dr. Lockhart thought the eye surgery would negatively affect Bertha and cause her to completely lose her mind.

But if she didn't have the cataract removed she would lose her sight. The family decided it was bad enough to have Daddy blind and told the doctor that Bertha just couldn't go blind, too. I told Dr. Lockhart, "We have faith in our God to help mother go through this eye surgery. We must take the chance."

Mother had her eye surgery operation in Richmond, Indiana. Judy and I sat with her for a whole week. We had some nurses come and give us a break at times. After Mom returned home it was not long before she began to walk out of the house in her slip not knowing what she was doing. Daddy couldn't see her and didn't know she was gone. The policemen found her and brought her home. It was then we knew we had to look into getting her in a nursing home.

14

The Nursing Home Years

✦

1968–1981

We moved Mother into the Smelser homestead in Connersville which had been bought by the Paula Mar nursing home. It was located at the bottom of 3rd Street hill on Western Avenue between 3rd & 4th St. She was only there a few weeks because we worried that she would fall down the stairs.

Judy found a brand new nursing home called the Golden Rule nursing home in Richmond, Indiana. Daddy decided since he was older now and he knew the State would pay for him to be in the nursing home so he would go, too. We knew that whatever assets they had would be used for their care. Daddy lived longer in the Summit Avenue house than he ever lived anywhere else. Bertha and George had lived there twenty-five years. On October 21, 1968 the State took over the Summit Avenue property and Mother and Dad moved to the Golden Rule nursing home. They lived there a few months and then returned back to Connersville to live at the Connersville Nursing Home which was located on Grand Avenue.

Looking back on the years of our parents care we feel our best efforts were made to help keep them in their home for as long as we possibly could. At least now they were in Connersville where family and friends could stop and visit with them without driving out of town. Dad's only handicap was being blind. He was very healthy, emotionally sound, excellent memory, and a real joy to those who knew him. Mother seems to adjust the best she could. They were able to share a room together for the remainder of those years.

Mother and Dad celebrated 50 years of marriage at a Golden Wedding Reception that was held at the home of Lowell and Judy Roettger in Rolling Green Estates north of Connersville. The open house party was in March 1970. Invitations were sent to family and friends and an announcement was published in the Connersville News Examiner. Many attended the party. My father sat in the front living room and greeted people throughout the day. George was 86 and Bertha was 73.

Mother's mental sickness caused her at times to lack an understanding of what was going on around her. She was not aware of what the celebration really meant. Still the gathering was very enjoyable for her. She especially liked the food and seemed like she just couldn't get enough to eat. Mother was dressed in a beautiful golden flowered dress I had picked out for her to wear for the occasion. Judy had taken her to a beauty shop to get her hair done. She was dressed in her new outfit and styled for the occasion. It was a wonderful day for her.

Bertha (Clark) Britton and George A. Britton on their 50th Wedding Anniversary 1970

My father preached every Sunday morning for about five years at the Connersville Nursing Home where he lived with Mother. Rosie came to play the piano and brought her accordion at times. It was often an occasion for a gathering of us kids just as we remember when we enjoyed our Sunday morning services many years ago at our home. We all loved serving the Lord in this nursing home ministry. Daddy preached straight from the Bible from his memory with a super sharp mind. The talents our parents had encouraged us to learn were helping us spread the gospel to those who lived here in the nursing home. We were united together not just as a family sharing the word of God to others but also as brothers and sisters in Christ.

Over the years of Sunday morning church services my father delivered to the residents of the nursing home we gave our praises though music, prayers, and

Bible lessons. Rosie's children would contribute their musical talents; Andy played the clarinet and Sylvia played the saxophone. Others would come and sing. I would help out at times directing the singing. Judy sang beautiful songs that added to the enjoyment of everyone. Most of us attended a church home one-half block north of the nursing home.

We would walk down after Sunday school and participate in George's services. We shared this participation and helped our father but mostly Rosie assisted Daddy in this ministry. After five years we decided that it was time for George to cut back to one Sunday every month.

At age eighty-nine, my father, a man of God, baptized a great granddaughter in one of the services. In fact this baby infant was my granddaughter, Katina Maria; it is a cherished memory.

Other preachers and lay witness leaders would come and visit George Britton for Bible studies, prayer and scripture reading. Many times leaving with rejoicing for the Christian fellowship that was shared through the witness of a humble blind man who lived for the Lord.

◆   ◆   ◆

Mother's mind continued to go, but she always knew us. She wasn't like an Alzheimer's patient who eventually doesn't remember or know much at all. The day before mother died Rosie had visited with her and she knew Rosie. Daddy was in the same room as mother. She was dying in the night and the nursing home people didn't tell Daddy. They took him out in the front lounge. Later after everything happened it grieved him to think he didn't get to be with mother during the last hours of her life. It was that morning when Daddy didn't hear mother and he went over to check on her and found a towel over her face. He uncovered her face and started to talk to her. It was then when a nurse came in and said, "Mr. Britton don't do that this will help her." I believe the nursing home put a towel over my mother's face so her breath would go sooner. Mother died July 14, 1973 at the age of 76, on Sunday morning.

When we went to the nursing home after my mother had passed away, they had gotten rid of her wheel chair and her golden wedding anniversary dress was missing. This was the treatment we got after all the things Daddy did at the nursing home. For years Daddy had conducted the Sunday morning church service. When there were patients that had special needs for comforting, the nurses would come and get George so he could go talk and pray with them. That was the thanks we got from that nursing home. I hated it with a passion. I had to turn it over to the Lord. Mother was buried in Dale Cemetery in the Britton plot.

My Grandmother Emma Mae (Fick) died in 1968 at the age of 96. Howard Clark my mother's brother was the last of her immediate family to die in 1992. He was 90.

◆   ◆   ◆

It was very soon afterwards that Rosie had Daddy moved over to the Lincoln Manor Nursing home on East 5th Street in Connersville. For eight years more Daddy lived to give us love, encouragement, and support. He was always our joy and strength in the times life would be difficult and when we would find ourselves in need of a person to listen.

George Britton's last sermon was preached on Father's Day when he was 93 years old at Gortner Memorial Nazarene Church West of Connersville. He was celebrating his Diamond Jubilee, 75 years of preaching and teaching the Gospel, since his first steps of faith which had begun at age 18.

Rosie was finishing her teaching career in Connersville at Eastview School which was located very close behind the Lincoln Manor. Often she would walk her 3rd grade class to the nursing home for a visit with a patriarch who could share wonderful stories about the land and God who made the land. The children were studying geography, learning about the earth surfaces, countries and about human life, too. George Britton told about his pioneering days in Canada and about the Indians. He knew how the land had been cleared by the hands of his pioneering parents; Hiram and Sarah, and their parents; Martin and Lucretia, who were his grandparents. He could tell them of all the rivers and the exploding of technology his generation had seen, from horse and buggy to cars and airplanes, to walking on the moon.

Daddy was there in the nursing home for us several more years. We would love to just visit and feel the comfort of his words. I asked him one time if it seemed like ninety seven years was a long time for him. He responded, "Not really. Time goes quite fast." Judy would come and visit with him. Beside his bed they would talk about things of the Lord and she would read the Bible to him. He often would speak to her, encouraging her to be the prayer leader for the family after his death. She explained to Daddy that her life was busy and that was too great of task for her to fulfill. Later Judy would realize that he wasn't just asking this of her.

Daddy died October 6, 1981 in his bed at the nursing home. He suffered no pain and went to sleep to wake in the Kingdom of Heaven to see his name written in God's Book of Life. He was the last one in his family of nine children to die; he was ninety seven years old. The day before his death Judy had visited with him. We had no idea that these last earthly requested words would be shared for us all to hand down over the generations to come. The passage of scriptures George Britton called upon was; Psalms 24; Psalms 23; Psalms 29: and the entire 14th Chapter of St. John. They are found in God's Holy Bible. We pray that you will take time to read these wonderful Bible verses and let them penetrate your very heart and soul.

Several years after the death of George Britton, Sarah Judy was in her home sewing when the Holy Spirit came upon her as she remembered what her father had asked her to do, which was pray for the generations past his death. Her heart began to listen to the message of the Spirit. George and Bertha had raised five children who all could be prayer warriors and leaders. She immediately phoned Rosie and through their discussions a family letter was started. Over the years, the letter has been written by the children and grandchildren of George and Bertha Britton.

Each year since the first letter which was written in 1988, it is sent to over one hundred families, to bring forth the Gospel and to tell others that they also can be saved through the redeeming blood of Jesus Christ the Son of God. It's our heritage for us to do this.

15

Bright Hopes for Tomorrow

❖

Present Day

The last of my father's sisters died in the same year 1976. Nellie died August 7, 1976 and her husband (Uncle Bob) Robert Grimes died on September 20, 1960. Elsie died November 9, 1976. Elsie and her husband Frank Lamb had retired to Tampa, Florida. My first trip to Florida was to see Aunt Elsie and Uncle Frank. They liked living in the warm climate and attended church. Frank died on December 18, 1953 in Tampa. Both sisters and their husbands are buried in the Dale Cemetery in the Britton plot.

If you visit the Dale Cemetery in Connersville you will be amazed to find the many graves of the ones who we have told about in this book. Many of the Clarks, Poe's and Britton's and even some of our younger family generation members are buried there. It was the wish of Hiram Britton and others that family plots were purchased so they would be buried close by to each other.

Many in our families believe that at the time of "The Rapture" the children of God who die in the faith of Jesus Christ will all be caught up in the twinkle of the eye in that glorious day of resurrection. We believe that our human bodies will be transformed into our eternal bodies and united in a life that will last forever. Won't it be a wonderful reunion when we all get to Heaven!

My brothers and sisters are retired and in good health. Death has taken some we love dearly but our faith and knowledge assures us that it is for only a short while until we reunite with those who have gone on to Heaven. We hold dear our memories of all the wonderful family times. There have been heartaches and sad unexplainable life events, but through it all how fortunate to have lived with Christian parents and in a home full of love. Love is something we had lot of in our home.

Land of Our Father; Land of Ours; A Land in which God created as our Father and The Land of Ours because we have believed.

THE END

To the beginning! Let the circle be unbroken for all God's Children.

Albert and Almeda live in Tucson, Arizona. They recently celebrated sixty years of marriage and are very well. They had six children; Sharon Rose, Phyllis Marie, Colleen Virginia, Philip Wayne, Kathleen Lois, and Ronald Albert. Philip Wayne Britton died September 20, 1971 as a result of being accidentally hit by a car as he was walking on the road. He was seventeen. Their children are all married. Several have children and some grandchildren. Albert and Almeda have worked serving in their local churches for many years witnessing and praying for the needs of all people. They are wonderful examples of how God wants us to grow together in Christ as husband and wife.

Rosie McKinney lives in Panama City, Florida and still gives everyday of her life in witness and in the service for God. She plays music and organizes services at a local senior citizen's meal site. Her strength comes from down within where God lives in her heart. Her eyes failed her for teaching full time towards the end but through the miracles of modern medicine and God her vision still remains. Rosie was inducted into the Fayette County School Corporation "Hall of Fame" in 2003. Her family is a treasure she has gained and brought her wonderful companionship. You can always be assured that Rosie is lifting many prayers on our behalf and she is loved. Rosie's children are Andy Francis, Roy Arthur, Sylvia Lois, and Gordon Charles. Andy Francis McKinney died December 9, 1994 at the age of thirty-nine years old. He was single and very musically talented. All of Rosie children are enjoying married life. She has several grandchildren.

Gordon and Vera Britton love the Lord and presently live in Richmond, Indiana. They have raised a fine family. Their five children are Carol Jo, Edward Gordon, Robert Dale, Belinda Jane, and William Arthur. They have all taken spouses and you can image how many Britton namesakes have come from Gordon and Vera. They have several grandchildren and now some great grandchildren. Gordon has been faithful to care for Vera who hasn't been well for sometime but still remains the lovely queenly lady from England who is dearly loved by all.

Our little sister, Judy means so much to us. Her husband, Lowell Roettger, lost his life in a short battle against cancer. He died on September 14, 1996. Their children are Randall Wayne, Daniel Lane, and Martin Edmund. Martin Edmund (Marty) Roettger died in a drowning accident at the age of two. Judy lives in Connersville at present. Randall and Daniel both are married raising children. Ryan Tyler Roettger the son of Randall is our special child in all the family. Ryan is crippled but has learned to be strong and of good courage. He is a fine 13 year old boy who has gone through many health challenges but God continues to answer prayers in his life.

I live with Herman in Panama City, Florida (at our place we call Windemere) in the winters and Connersville, Indiana in the warm seasons. Everyday we praise the Lord for His Blessings. This last year Herman was baptized, joined the church, gave witness of his faith in Jesus Christ just before his 82nd Birthday. We have three children; David George, Rita Ann, and Dennis Joseph. David and Rita are married and have grown children and grandchildren. Joe has never married but was awarded a silver pin on his 25th anniversary of recognition of being a licensed Medical Lab Technician.

I retired from Dr. John W. Reichle DDS in 1986 where I had worked since 1963. I did some interesting work for the IRS in Covington, Kentucky for a short time period. I enjoy my grown grandchildren and now my great grandchildren. Keeping up with two houses, I find myself busy all the time. Retirement gives us days to do what we choose and mine are filled with hectic moments sprinkled with television and corresponding with friends and family. I like to travel, sew, and do nice things for people. Rita and I have kept the phone lines and email going with questions and conversations concerning the writings in this book. We pray for all the family needs and worship regularly.

We want to thank everyone for their support and patience in the writing of this book, for the time we spent interviewing and asking for stories you all remember and some you do not remember. Roberta (Grimes) Rush passed away this year February 2004. She contributed to this book, too. Thanks to Vincent Britton who encouraged the progress of the book as he was stationed in the Iraq War April 2003. Especially to Benjamin (Ben) King we say, "Thank you!" He has supported Rita throughout this endeavor since she began this project in 2001 and his editing talents that put the finishing touch on this book. It is a pleasure to be part of a loving family.

The way the Lord has kept us in the past, that's the way he's going to keep us in the future. Bright Hopes for Tomorrow with Christ's love to you all.

Written by Aunt Grace Britton   *1895–1961*

The Day after Christmas at Grandma's

Twas the Day after Christmas
And all through the house
Not a thing was in place
Not even our mouse.
And mom with her dust pan
And I with the broom
Must sweep and clean
And scour every room.

Christmas morn the floors
Was so clean and so neat
But now bears the marks
Of twelve pair of feet.
The chairs sticky with candy
Look out for your pants
If you sit down you're stuck
There isn't a chance.

The windows are smeared
You can hardly see through
The organ is daubed with pie and cake, too.
And popcorn and raisins
All stuck in the rug
And no end of the dirt
So far as we've dug.

Who did all of this?
Why the Grandchildren dear
They come home for Christmas
Once every year.
But they had a good time
So I'll not say a thing
Till Christmas comes again
The Grandchildren to bring.

Written in the early 1920's.
Later there were 24 Grandchildren in all

105

Endnotes

1. "The Histories of Several Communities in Pendleton County, Kentucky" Mildred Bowen Belew author internet article

2. The Rush to Oklahoma; John W. Reps, Professor Emeritus, Cornell University, Ithaca, New York, web document

3. Our Glorious Century; Reader's Digest 1994

4. McKercher, Robert B., and Wolf, Bertram (1986). Understanding Western Canada's Dominion Land Survey System. Division of Extension and Community Relations, University of Saskatchewan.

5. Connersville Times, Wednesday, March 30, 1887, Local Matters A.S. Clark death notice.

6. Connersville A Pictorial History, Harry M. Smith, 1992

7. Cincinnati Enquirer, Rivers Unleashed, Web Publication 2003

0-595-34094-6